QUEEN TAKE YOUR THRONE

QUEEN TAKE YOUR THRONE

EVERY WOMAN'S CALL TO AUTHORITY

EILEEN WALLIS

PUBLISHING

COLUMBIA, MISSOURI

Unless otherwise indicated, all Scripture quotations are from the Holy Bible, New International Version, ©1973, 1978, 1984 International Bible Society. Used by permission of Zondervan Bible Publishers.

Verses so indicated are taken from The Living Bible, copyright 1971 by Tyndale House Publisher, Wheaton, Ill. Used by permission.

Verses marked (NKJV) are taken from The New King James Version. Copyright © 1979, 1980, 1982, Thomas Nelson, Inc., Publishers.

Cover design by Jan Petersen

Printed in the United States of America

ISBN 0-939159-04-X

Published by Cityhill Publishing
A division of Christian Fellowship of Columbia
4600 Christian Fellowship Road
Columbia, Mo. 65203

CONTENTS

FOREWORD

In recent decades our society has undergone a revolution in its thinking about women. Their status has been elevated, and progress is continuing in several areas. Much of this has been good.

But commending the progress of women doesn't mean we agree with the declared intentions of the women's liberation movement: to make the sexes equal in every respect. The plain fact is that God has not made men and women equal. If you compare gifts and abilities, many women can outmatch men. But in God's kingdom, ability does not equal government. People use the wrong terms when they speak of one sex being superior or inferior to the other. Neither gender is better; they're just different. Women have different roles to play, different contributions to make, and often different gifts to exercise than men. The contributions of men and of women are equally valuable, equally necessary.

In homes where women do the driving and men take the back seat, the husband, not the wife, is often to blame. He has ducked his God-given responsibility. I once asked a wife why she always made the major family decisions. She replied, "I really want to submit to my husband. I just wish he would give me something to submit to!"

In homes and churches where God's order prevails — where men lovingly and firmly take leadership and women submit without being stifled or suppressed — there is harmony and security. Leadership always remains weak until God's order is established.

The strong emphasis in the past on the man's authority has been necessary. But it's easy to emphasize that truth so much that there's little room for women to exercise their God-given ministry. That results in incalculable loss for the kingdom of God.

Sometimes people get the impression that the husband should exercise the authority and the only thing to look for in a wife is submission. This has deepened women's feelings of inferiority and confirmed Satan's lie, which all too many women have embraced, that they are second-class citizens in God's kingdom. Some women with great abilities become frustrated when they feel they can't use their gifts in the local church. So they look elsewhere for a place where they can function with greater freedom.

My wife, Eileen, draws from the story of Esther to show that every believing woman is called to be a queen. This is no empty, artificial title, a sop to make deprived women feel good. This is no carnival queen who basks in her moment of glory before sinking back into oblivion. Her authority is for real and for life. Just what that authority is and how it works for women, whether single or married, is laid out here in simple, practical terms.

Rightly used, the woman's authority will never undermine or threaten that of the man. The queen's throne is to complement, not compete with, that of the king. It is because too many queens' thrones remain unoccupied that many men are not as secure and as fruitful as they should be. When women of God reign in life, they challenge and stir men to do the same.

I've shared my life with the author for thirty-eight years. I'm in a position to testify that she is not merely preaching a message, but sharing what has been over these years a growing reality in her own life. It works for her. It can work for you.

Arthur Wallis

PREFACE

The idea for this book — applying the biblical story of Queen Esther to modern women's roles — began as a seed thought. It was watered and grew as I shared my ideas with others, especially friends in the United States. When they first encouraged me to write a book, I was incredulous. My husband, Arthur, was the writer, not me! I'm especially grateful for the early interest shown by Barbara Sullivan of Chicago and Kent Garborg of Minneapolis. When my husband counseled me to seek God about writing the book, I realized it was a challenge I could not lightly dismiss.

I had always enjoyed helping my husband with his writing ministry, even the tedious task of proofreading manuscripts. Little did I realize that those years had been preparing me to put pen to paper myself.

Now with the task accomplished, much of the credit must go to Arthur, my tutor, supporter, and encourager. He patiently helped me apply myself to the discipline of sitting at a desk to write. Like most women, I much prefer activity and variety.

Nor could I have succeeded without the prayers and help of many friends, especially those in my church, the Community Church in Southampton, England. Diana Moss deserves my special thanks for so efficiently typing the manuscript. I also feel a debt of thanks for the many American women who have blessed me with their love and inspired me with their enthusiasm for God.

Before beginning the first chapter of *Queen Take Your Throne*, I encourage you to read the Book of Esther. Pray that it will come alive to you. If you enjoy Bible study, I hope you'll find the study questions at each chapter's end stimulating. They were designed so you can use them on your own or in a group setting. It's my prayer that this book will help you gain the vision and faith you need to take your throne.

1

THE QUEEN IN VIEW

It was 4 a.m. I arose and scurried to board a train on the outskirts of London. The sky was still black when my friends and I reached the heart of the city. Crowds were already forming. Some eager spectators had come the previous night to insure themselves a good view. Their sleeping bags and blankets were still strewn along the sidewalks. By daybreak, tens of thousands of people were pouring into the capital.

Forty years have passed since that thrilling November day. It's still etched like a commemorative coin upon my memory. The event was the wedding of Prince Philip and Princess Elizabeth. All of Great Britain had anticipated the happy occasion, and everyone was in high spirits. People especially wanted a glimpse of the bride. She was the oldest child of King George VI and heir to the throne of England.

People lined the route of the royal procession. It would begin at Buckingham Palace, travel to Westminster Abbey for the ceremony, then return to the palace. There was no television in those days, and loudspeakers were hung from light posts along the way so everyone could hear the ceremony.

The crowd thickened throughout the morning until people could barely move. Parents passed little children over heads to the front, where they could get a better view under the watchful eye of the policemen lining the street. Late in the morning, cars filled with wedding guests began passing on their way to the ceremony. People would shout and applaud when they spotted a celebrity. The anticipation mounted with each passing car.

Then, at last, Elizabeth came into view. She was riding in an open carriage pulled by four steeds with uniformed riders. The crowd erupted in shouts, claps, and cheers. She was a striking sight with her tiara and beautifully bejeweled and embroidered gown. She was escorted by a guard of cavalry famed for its expert riding. They wore bright gold and red uniforms, and the white plumes on their hats bobbed as the horses trotted past.

Prince Philip looked dashing in his naval dress uniform. He rode to the wedding in a separate coach. Then came the royal families, also in horse-drawn carriages, followed by a string of long, gleaming Rolls Royce limousines. They carried dignitaries and heads of state.

My friends and I stood about a quarter of a mile from Westminster Abbey. We could hear the roar of the crowd when the newlyweds stepped out of the cathedral. The thundering cheers drew nearer; the couple's carriage passed within a few yards of us. We stood in awe. Waving to us was a 21-year-old woman who would one day reign over the British Empire. Little did we realize how soon that would be. Within five years, King George died and Elizabeth took the throne.

Queens are rare these days. They're often regarded as figureheads of pageantry remote from the real world. But even so, they have an enduring mystique.

Queen Elizabeth has lived in a global spotlight since age nine, when she became heir to the throne. People have always been fascinated with her life and family. Media from China to Canada monitor their every move; books written about them become bestsellers. Now a new generation has arisen, and Prince Charles, the next heir, and his wife, Princess Diana, are also making front-page headlines wherever they go.

What sparks so much interest in royalty? Why is the queen regarded with such respect? Whether meeting schoolchildren or diplomats, the queen is always expected to be poised and gracious. How embarrassed Britons would be if the queen didn't dress and act with the dignity suiting her position.

Why do people feel this way about a queen?

I believe something deep inside us all wants to see a nation or kingdom represented with honor. A crown represents a responsibility to live according to a high standard of integrity. Britons expect the royal family to live above reproach and to set an example. British citizens have high ideals for their country, and they expect the queen to uphold those standards.

Scripture teaches that Christians, like royalty, are heirs and representatives of the kingdom of God. We have the high calling of demonstrating life in Christ to the watching world. God has appointed His people as the only examples on earth of His government, His way of life. We have all been chosen to exercise the authority of His crown.

The British monarch, in particular, serves as an apt illustration of the authority God has granted women. The queen of England reigns, but she does not rule. She doesn't govern Britain, but she represents the nation. She reigns through her authority and influence, but the final authority rests elsewhere: with the British Parliament.

The women of God represent Christ's kingdom of righteousness, peace, and joy. They were chosen to reign in that kingdom, but they don't rule over their husbands or church leaders. They exercise great influence for godliness, but rulership has been delegated to men.

In Britain, an unwritten understanding of mutual respect allows the queen to exercise her influence without usurping the power of Parliament. Officially, Parliament cannot act without the queen's signature. But she defers to the will of the people as vested in Parliament. She does not govern, but her influence extends to the government. The queen is called upon to cast the tie-breaking vote, for example, if Parliament is deadlocked on the choice of a prime minister.

The law doesn't compel anyone to do as the queen says. But, by virtue of her position, she wields quiet power. People listen to the queen and take her wishes seriously. Notables and leaders in every field — business, science, literature, the arts — treasure an audience with the queen. The British prime minister traditionally meets with her weekly for a private discussion. Regardless of their political affiliation, the prime ministers have looked forward to these conversations and have respected the queen's well-informed opinions. The queen is regarded by many as Britain's most knowledgeable diplomat because of her longtime relationships with foreign leaders.

The queen's influence on ordinary citizens stems partly from her willingness to live her life in public view. Rather than riding in the safe seclusion of a bullet-proof limousine, she travels in an open vehicle. Rather than remaining aloof in the palace, she goes on "walkabouts," casual strolls in which she mingles freely with shop-keepers and people on the street. "I have to be seen to be believed," she once remarked.

The queen's desire is to serve her nation and its people. Her life is devoted to that purpose. Whether she watches a soccer match, visits a new housing project, or inspects a factory, she talks to people and takes an interest in their work. People feel that what they're doing is worthwhile because the queen has taken an interest in it.

Likewise, a woman who is walking with God has an enormous influence on the men and women around her. She doesn't remain proudly aloof, but humbly identifies with people at their point of need. People from all walks of life respect her and want to hear what she has to say. They take special interest in how she handles her affairs. Other Christians regard her as an example to follow because in her they see Christ. It's His touch upon her life that gives her authority to act on His behalf. She receives authority because of who she is in Christ.

Too often Christian women don't think of themselves as daughters of the King of Kings, full heirs in the greatest kingdom of all. Instead of experiencing confidence, many Christian women are dogged by feelings of worthlessness and inferiority. They regard themselves as second-class citizens rather than as members of the royal household.

Part of this negative image has been created by worldly pressures to devalue the traditional role of the wife, mother, and home-maker. The world says that a woman's identity and value must come from a career or some other outside accomplishment and that ordinary household tasks have nothing to do with feminine fulfillment.

These doubts of self-worth have been reinforced by unbalanced teaching on submission in some Christian circles. Submission was strongly stressed because women had begun dominating in churches where men were prone to sit back and watch. Some domineering women relished the opportunity to run the show. Many others were genuinely spiritual women who simply desired to see their churches move forward. As men abdicated more responsibility, women called the shots. The result: churches were out of order.

Against this backdrop, God's Spirit began to move. Men saw the emerging problems and began taking the lead in their homes and churches. Teaching on the truths of submission prompted women to step aside so men could assume their rightful place. But as so easily happens in other areas, this teaching evolved into legalism. Leaders of women's Bible studies would sum up the role of the Christian woman: "You must submit. It's in the Bible." That was it. The law of submission.

Is that the Spirit of Christ? Does that really sum up biblical teaching on a woman's role? Where does grace operate? Where's the liberty for which Christ has set us free?

Uncertain of their proper domain, Christian women retreated from ministry. Better to sit on the sidelines and do nothing than to play too big a part. After all, how can a godly woman follow the scriptural command to be submissive and still have a powerful, life-changing influence on people's lives? That wouldn't be scriptural. Or would it?

The women of a church in London a few years ago wondered a lot about their proper role. They were sure of only one thing: they didn't want to usurp the authority of men. The pastor and other men in leadership had no qualms about women giving testimonies, praying, or prophesying in a service, but women were holding back from these things, unsure of their proper place. Some even felt apprehensive about women taking charge of women's gatherings.

In December 1983, the leaders' wives were praying together about plans for an upcoming women's meeting. One of them, deep in prayer, saw a picture come into her mind. She was standing before a gaily decorated Christmas tree surrounded with gift-wrapped packages. The woman picked up one package and noticed the label.

"Authority," it read. She quickly put it back.

"That's not for me," she said to herself. "That's for the men."

She shared this mental picture with the group. It puzzled them. Authority, it seemed, was only for men. What did authority have to do with women? Was this a sign that women were overstepping their bounds? Or did it mean the opposite, that women had been shrinking from responsibilities that God had intended for them? Perhaps God wanted them to minister with more authority. But doesn't authority imply domination? They left wondering if God were preparing them for a fresh understanding of the role of women in the church.

I knew nothing of this when, a month later, I came to speak at the women's meeting about which they had been praying. My topic was the Book of Esther. The central figure in this fascinating story is not the Persian king or his chief male official. It's a woman, Esther. Her life altered the history of a nation. She wasn't a domineering or aggressive woman; in fact, she exemplified a meek, gentle, submissive spirit. Yet God chose her for a position of authority.

As the story unfolded, these women found answers for their situation. They found that authority isn't taking rulership. It's functioning in your God-given abilities in a way that demonstrates His authority. They went away more confident, encouraged, and ready to function in a new dimension of liberty and faith.

Queen Take Your Throne tells how a Jewish orphan girl became a queen and how her life applies to you, God's woman. Like so many other Christian women, you may be feeling insignificant and inferior to others. Some of you may hold no place of prominence from which to draw self-esteem. Perhaps you have no high-powered job. You're not the pastor's wife or the head of the Sunday school. You don't sing special music. Much of your time may be occupied with mundane tasks: punching a cash register, filing papers, checking groceries, babysitting, cleaning the house, wiping runny noses, doing laundry. How can you feel like what you're doing is worthwhile?

It's time to discover who you are and to step out in faith on the royal road to fulfillment.

STUDY QUESTIONS
THE SOURCE OF OUR AUTHORITY

Authority exercised by men and women in the body of Christ has nothing to do with authoritarianism, which Webster defines as "favoring blind submission to authority." Rather, authority is the power to influence thought, opinion, or behavior.

Godly women are to exercise this kind of authority for the glory of God and the extension of His kingdom. This is God-given authority. We don't possess it ourselves or receive it by holding an influential position.

1. Read Matthew 28:18-20 and Ephesians 1:18-22.
   What is the source of authority?
   How much authority does Jesus have?
   Where does His authority come from?
   For what purpose do we receive this authority?
2. Read Luke 24:49; Acts 1:8; and Acts 2:4.
   What happened when Jesus' disciples received "power from on high"? Were women there, too?
3. Read Matthew 8:5-10.
   In this passage, the Roman centurion recognized that Jesus had authority. He also understood that He had authority because He had met one condition. What was that condition? (See verse 9.)

2

REVOLT REVEALED

The capital of Persia was bursting with the news. King Xerxes had announced a celebration that would awe the world. It was to last *six months*. The guest list was most impressive: princes, noblemen, governors, generals, dignitaries. Representatives would come from each of the empire's 127 provinces. The entourage would number in the thousands.

The king had a grand purpose in mind. After ruling the Persian Empire for three years, he wanted to display the vast wealth and splendor of his kingdom, which sprawled across parts of Asia, Africa, the Middle East, and Europe. Total power was vested in him alone. The king would gather the most skilled craftsmen and the finest goods from India to Ethiopia to show the world his majesty.

Susa, the magnificent capital city, was a fitting site. The thriving commercial center was set in a lush river valley with a delightful climate. Rising high above the valley was the beautiful palace citadel with its richly adorned halls and throne room.*

The king must have been greatly appreciative of the people's efforts to make the first celebration such a success. After the guests departed, he invited the entire city to a week-long banquet in the palace gardens. Everyone from the poorest farmer to the wealthiest merchant enjoyed the king's generosity. Queen Vashti undoubtedly

---

* Editor's note: In 1852, a French archaeological expedition began excavating ancient Susa, beside the Shawur river in modern-day Iran. The expedition discovered a city covering eight square miles, as well as the huge palace of King Xerxes (486-465 B.C.), who ruled at the height of the Persian Empire. The features of the city and palace, including the king's throne room, match those described in the Book of Esther.

had a key role in planning the arrangements for this colossal event. The king could not have managed well without her. Her beauty and grace were valuable assets as the royal couple welcomed dignitaries together, showing visiting political leaders and military commanders what it was like to be part of such a magnificent kingdom.

The gardens were decorated with blue and white linens fastened with silver rings to the massive marble pillars. The townspeople sat on couches of gold and silver and walked on mosaic floors of marble, pearl, and costly stones. Everyone ate in abundance and drank as much as they wished. Wine was served in golden goblets, each uniquely crafted.

Queen Vashti was given the privilege of arranging a special banquet for the ladies. She became the center of attention as she took charge of the festivities. She knew that the women would not overlook anything. They would scrutinize her choice of clothes, food, decorations, and her every word and action. Every detail had to be perfect.

The women's banquet was held on the final day of the celebration, and Vashti was in the limelight. The women were having a splendid time enjoying the entertainment and festivities that Vashti had planned so well. Then there came an unexpected interruption. Seven couriers arrived from the king. They carried a message for the queen. King Xerxes wanted Vashti to leave the banquet and join him, arrayed in her crown and royal robes. He wanted to introduce her to his guests.

But, surrounded by all these admiring women, Vashti was enjoying herself. She didn't want to leave. This new-found authority had swollen her pride.

"No!" she snapped at the couriers. She ignored their request and went on with her banquet.

The king was furious. With one thoughtless act, his wife had not only humiliated him, but had undermined all his efforts to display his majesty. She had demonstrated rebellion and independence before a huge crowd of watching women. They looked to her as their example. This incident was bound to affect their behavior toward their own husbands.

Besides, what was the point of showing how powerful he was if

Xerxes couldn't even command the obedience and respect of his own wife? News of this would travel quickly to all corners of the empire. Something had to be done immediately.

The test had come, and Vashti had proven unfit. The moment she refused to obey, she lost the right to reign. She failed in the very purpose for which she had been given authority. What began as eagerness to carry out the king's wishes turned into selfishness.

Despite his anger, the king responded with great restraint. He made no hasty decision. He first consulted his wisest counselors, who were concerned that justice be done. Vashti had not only offended her husband, but had wronged every household in Persia. Vashti had to accept responsibility for her actions as queen.

The verdict was inevitable. The crown was taken from her; it would be given to someone more worthy. Vashti was barred forever from the king's presence.

Vashti had just gotten what she wanted all along: independence. She wanted to do her own thing. When the choice came whether to please the king or please herself, she chose herself.

How could the king trust her after she had shown such disrespect? With insolence there could be no harmony. Families would be disrupted wherever wives followed Vashti's example. There would be no end to the disrespect and discord. The king sent an edict to the people throughout Persia, translated into each of the many languages. It proclaimed that every man should be ruler of his own household. Another queen would need to be found, but not until the men were once again firmly in control.

When someone in a prominent position rebels, it's obvious to everyone. Vashti's faults could not be hidden. Our rebellion may not be so evident, but the lesson still applies.

Rebellion is choosing to follow your own ideas rather than those of the people above you: your husband, pastor, teacher, boss. Some women get along fine as long as they're happy with what they're being asked to do. But they launch a palace revolt whenever they think they have a better way. We're free to disagree and express our opinions. But when our opinions have been overruled, we need to accept that decision.

Rebellion is always against God; we're resentful or angry about the circumstances and people He's placed in our lives. But that rebellion shows up in our relationships with people. We choose self-will rather than acknowledging the authority of those God has placed over us and choosing to live in harmony with them.

Complaining and arguing are signs of rebellion. They are the soils in which the seed of rebellion can flourish. The children of Israel began grumbling in the desert when they came to a place where there was no water. Before long, they were questioning God's presence and were ready to stone Moses.[1]

The Bible makes it clear that rebellion is a serious offense to God. The prophet Samuel told King Saul, "Rebellion is as the sin of witchcraft, and stubbornness is as iniquity and idolatry."[2]

We can demonstrate the beauty and glory of God's kingdom only if we're free from the rebellion that ruined Vashti. She lived in an age vastly different from our own, yet the same traits are evident in women today. Attitudes of rebellion will disqualify you from becoming a woman of influence in God's kingdom. Recognizing these attitudes in yourself is the first step to being released from them.

STUDY QUESTIONS
WOMEN OF INFLUENCE

1. Read Esther 1: 9-18. How many people were influenced by Vashti's behavior? In what way did she influence them?
2. Write down the names of all the people you are influencing by your life.
3. Christians are to be the "aroma of Christ." See 2 Corinthians 2:15. How many Scriptures can you find that show how you can be an influence that spreads the wonderful fragrance of life?

   Here are some examples:
   • By your speech (Col. 4:16)
   • By the way you work (Col. 3:23-24)
   • By your attitude (Phil. 2:3)
   • By your actions (1 Peter 3:8-9)

3

THE LIBERATED WOMAN

Vashti looked lovely. As far as we know that was the only reason she had been given the crown. The king saw how beautiful she was and decided she was worthy of honor. Her crown was a recognition of the beauty of her womanhood. No man could wear that crown; it was a woman's privilege.

It's a privilege to be a woman because God has endowed us with beautiful qualities worthy of honor. The woman's touch is something of which to be proud, a gift with which to serve others. We bring the warmth and caring qualities of womanhood wherever we go. Some women can artfully transform the plainest of homes into beauty with a handful of flowers. God designed womanhood to be attractive; our outward appearance is seen at its best when accompanied by beauty of character.

The king expected Vashti to be a woman whose character matched her beauty. Who else would make a worthy queen? Early on, he had no reason to suspect any flaw. Outwardly she was a model of how a queen should behave. But her lovely appearance camouflaged the hidden traits of self-will and rebellion. Then came the fateful day when the king wanted others to see the woman he had chosen.

It was then the camouflage was torn away and Vashti's true self revealed. In one blatant, rebellious act, she threw away her crown. She had tasted new power by taking charge of the women's banquet. She had discovered how far-reaching her influence could be. But she had thought to herself, "With all this queenly authority, why should I defer to my husband's wishes? Why be *just* a woman?" Vashti was despising her greatest asset: her womanhood.

In so doing, she lost a vital opportunity to influence men as well

23

as women. As the realm's most prominent woman, Vashti could have challenged the men to be better men, worthy of their women.

What we are as women either corrupts or inspires the men in our lives. Eve influenced Adam to disobey God.[1]   Solomon's wives turned his heart away from God.[2] Deborah rallied the nation of Israel to victory.[3]   Timothy's mother and grandmother inspired him to become a man of faith.[4]

Scripture teaches that submission is not weakness but the most powerful influence a woman can exert. Peter said that wives would win their unbelieving husbands to the Lord just by their purity and reverence.[5] God desires to set us free from thinking of submission as a straitjacket. If we see submission as a legalistic duty, we feel hemmed in, stifled, unable to express ourselves. And we become vulnerable to the suggestion that a woman is second-rate.

Submission is not meant to squelch or inhibit you, but to bring you into the authority that allows you to freely function at your highest potential. We exercise *authority* by carrying out the King's commands. No man or woman has authority in the kingdom unless he or she comes under the headship of Christ. He is the supreme example of submission.

"During the days of Jesus' life on earth," Scripture says, "he offered up prayers and petitions with loud cries and tears to the one who could save him from death, and he was heard because of his reverent submission."[6] In the Gospel of John, Jesus says: "I tell you the truth, the Son can do nothing by himself; he can do only what he sees his Father doing, because whatever the Father does the Son also does."[7]

Jesus, who submitted to His Father in everything, manifested all the power and glory of the Godhead. For you, great freedom will come with the revelation that submission isn't meant to be an oppressive obligation. When you submit, as Christ did, you'll find the straitjacket was just in your mind.

This was the case with a friend of mine, whom I'll call Ann. Like many young mothers, she was pressured by family circumstances. She had two small children and felt like a shut-in. She seemingly had no escape from the constant demands. She longed for independence. She longed for a change. She badly wanted to return to her former job as a nurse, on a part-time basis.

It all sounded so reasonable as she talked it over with her husband. The children would enjoy having their father to look after them when Ann came home to sleep after her night shifts. She was sure she could cope, sure no one would suffer. The family would benefit from the extra money. Her husband was agreeable. But they decided to discuss it with an elder of their church and his wife, with whom they were friends. The couple offered no reservations.

Ann was delighted at the prospect of being back in her old job once more. She had the blessing of her husband and a church elder; how much better than acting on her own. She felt spiritually alive as she started the job. It was great to taste the freedom from the chores at home for a while each week.

At first, everything went well. Then the strain began to show on her family. Her job had added an extra burden and pressure on her husband. That was causing problems. Ann brushed aside any suggestion that her job was proving to be too much for her family. She was confident she was doing the right thing and all would be well. But the conflict became obvious to the elder and his wife. They counseled Ann to either give up the job or cut her hours severely.

Ann was indignant. She couldn't understand this advice. She had submitted the matter to them in the first place, so she felt she was right in continuing. She kept arguing and finding ways to justify her actions. She found herself resenting her husband and friends and became unable to listen to them.

A miserable week followed. The elation she had felt over her new job had burst like a balloon. Her spiritual life plummeted, and her heart began to long for the joy and peace she once knew. Her husband suggested she seek the Lord about it and hear herself what He had to say. She was willing.

As Ann knelt before the Lord, the questions came flooding in. How much does this job mean to you? Aren't your family and your life in God much more important? She knew the answers. The moment she said, "Yes, Lord!" peace came flooding back. No longer did Ann want to go her own way.

Ann gladly gave up her nursing job. To her amazement she found that her whole attitude had changed. She couldn't understand why she had ever been so stubborn. By allowing Ann to have her own way, while she was seemingly submitted to others, God had laid the groundwork for the real test.

She wanted to be free and had found it in her own way. But this freedom was short-lived and ended in misery. God was working to release her from the idea that she had to escape her situation and do something else to find fulfillment. Instead, she found freedom in completely embracing her role as a mother and wife and seeing its value. Once her attitude changed, she really began to enjoy herself. When her heart gladly said no to herself and accepted God's will for her, she found a new and lasting freedom. This is always the fruit of heartfelt submission.

This is not to say that every working mother is in the same position. The issues of a wife's job or career are something that husbands and wives must work out together. Women just need to put the Lord and their families first. But in making these decisions, beware of listening to the world's deception: "Instead of staying at home, why don't you do something, be something?" The hidden message is that it's of no value to raise children and be a supportive wife and homemaker. Don't believe it for a minute.

The symptoms of rebellion are woven into the fabric of human nature. They affect us all. Open rebellion is easy to diagnose and to condemn. But we need to be alert for its more subtle forms, especially those that undermine our ability to enjoy our womanhood. Sometimes young women have told me how much they are looking forward to marriage. Then in almost the same breath they have declared, "But I don't want to lose my identity and my independence."

Such a statement springs from a false concept of marriage. We don't lose our identity but find a new one. An independent spirit will rob a woman of finding this new identity, which can be experienced only by living in genuine harmony with her husband. Those who cling to their independence tread on dangerous ground. They are following the Vashti trail.

It's so easy to make unhappy circumstances an excuse for rebellion. A woman I'll call Helen followed that route. She strongly resented the way her father had tyrannized her mother. She left home determined never to be dominated by any man. Her happy marriage to a loving husband was not enough to root out this attitude and the accompanying fear.

Her life was up and down like a mountain trail. She and her husband went through troubled times in their relationship. Their spiritual lives were lacking as well. Like so many other couples, it seemed as if they could never make it together. When one was up, the other was always down.

Whenever her husband went through a difficult period, Helen amazed us all by the way she coped. She seemed to be spiritually strong and the mainstay of her family. Throughout these times, she felt secure in God. But when her husband was walking closer with the Lord, Helen found herself feeling insecure and battling the old problems.

The answer lay deep within her. In her heart, she could not truly submit to her husband. As long as he was away from God, she could take charge. But once he was restored, the old fear of domination took over. This, in turn, opened the door once more to the rebellion that was sapping her spiritual life.

The cycle was finally interrupted when Helen recognized her need to be freed from the Vashti view of freedom and independence.

Though God had used Helen and her husband as individuals, He wanted to use them in a much greater way as a team. They became instruments of blessing to others who were struggling with similar difficulties. It all hinged on Helen overcoming her fear and trusting God. When she no longer saw biblical submission as a smothering straitjacket, she could take her rightful place alongside her husband.

STUDY QUESTIONS
BEAUTY OF CHARACTER

Vashti's outward beauty became a veneer hiding the defects of her character. We are not all naturally beautiful, but in Christ we are called to develop a beautiful character. Our outward appearance should reflect an inward reality. Second Corinthians 5:17 tells us who we really are.

1. Read John 15:1-8. Character is the product of our relation-

ship with Christ. What does it mean to remain in or abide in
Christ?

2. Name some character qualities or "fruits" that Christians are
   to produce. Begin by looking at the list in Galatians 5:22-26.

3. Some women take too much pride in their appearance. Others
   think it's unspiritual to bother about how they look. How can
   we strike a healthy balance? Look for the answer in the above
   Scriptures as well as others.

4

MADE MAJESTIC TOGETHER

A great throng of people scurried to prepare for the six-month festival. It took months to build and furnish the lavish guest quarters. Gold, silver, and precious stones were gathered from across the empire.

Then, when the festival got underway, thousands of workers were needed to arrange the festivities and attend to the guests: musicians, entertainers, cooks, waitresses, maids, laundry workers, seamstresses, grooms for the horses.

All this was part of King Xerxes' campaign to display the wealth and majesty of his kingdom. The Lord likewise has ordained a campaign to put the majesty of His eternal kingdom on display so that people might be drawn to Him.[1]

Just as King Xerxes couldn't display the greatness of his kingdom single-handedly, Christians cannot display the Lord's splendor and magnitude alone. It's much too big a task for us as individuals. That is why God says: "You are a chosen people, a royal priesthood, a holy nation, a people belonging to God, that you may declare the praises of him who called you out of darkness into his wonderful light."[2] All those in the world who encounter God's people — government authorities, employers, relatives — are going to have the glory of God demonstrated before their eyes.

God has determined that His glory would be reflected through His body — the church — and through the relationships within it. But with whom can we have these relationships? Granted, we need to weep with the suffering church in China and pray for the persecuted Christians behind the Iron Curtain. But long-distance concern for brethren we've never met doesn't meet the needs of those near at hand.

God's commandment to love one another has practical implications. We can't dismiss it by claiming to love the worldwide family of believers while remaining isolated in our own communities. God intends for each believer to join with others in a local church to create a showcase of His way of life. We're instructed to have relationships with one another and to not give up meeting together.[3]

During the first twenty years of our marriage my husband was a full-time itinerant speaker at churches, conferences, and other gatherings. In a sense, he was accountable to no one. We served the Lord and thought we answered to Him alone.

Then the Lord began to speak to Arthur about the need for relationships with other traveling ministers. So they began meeting and praying together. They saw the need to share their lives and to support and encourage one another. They also saw the need to be accountable, not in a legalistic way, but in the context of loving relationships.

Out of this small beginning in 1972 grew what is now known in Britain as the restoration movement, which seeks to restore the principles of the New Testament church. Hundreds of "restoration" churches have emerged, comprising the fastest growing segment of Christianity in Great Britain.

During our years of independence we served the Lord earnestly and looked to Him alone for all our needs. Now, looking back, we realize how much we were missing. Arthur and I have found we can be more fruitful and function more effectively when we're knit together with others who share our vision.

Christians can serve God earnestly, wholeheartedly, even sacrificially, yet remain independent. God sees our hearts and delights to use us, but it's not His best. The sun is setting on the days of the "Lone Ranger" Christian. All across the globe the Lord is saying, "Get together."

God has called us to join together as a people and demonstrate His alternative way of life. There's no better way to accomplish this than to follow God's simple plan of using the local church. By doing so, we form the ranks of a mighty army establishing His rule on earth. Single soldiers engaged in their own skirmishes are no threat to Satan. But God's army is invincible.

In 1984 the story of a terribly injured farm worker in Hampshire

County appeared in several national newspapers in England. Something went awry as this fellow was working, and a farm machine severed his arm from his body. He had the presence of mind to pick it up and run with it a half mile to a farmhouse. He collapsed there and was found and rushed to a hospital. Doctors performed surgery for eight hours in a stunning attempt to attach the lifeless nerves and tissues to the body.

When the arm was apart from the body it was useless. But because of the surgeons' skill in rejoining it, there was hope of regaining use of the arm. What a lesson this has for Christians. We are all vital, living organs and tissues in Christ's body on earth.[4] He is the head, and we are eyes, ears, hearts, hands. Together we make up the whole body. Each one of us has a valuable part to play. But to function effectively we must be joined together.

All born-again believers are part of the universal church. But Christians miss out when they're not part of the local expression of the body of Christ. That's where we can love not with words but with actions.[5]

Jesus prayed that His body would be one.[6] He said this was the best way to advertise His kingdom and reach the world.[7] We sing about it, and we know it's going to happen because Jesus prayed for it. But we can also do something about it. We may not be able to heal all the divisions in the worldwide church, but we can display our unity in a local church where our neighbors can see us loving and helping one another. When they see it, they'll want to be part of it.

In 1974 my husband and I moved to a nearby town. About a dozen men and women from our church turned out to give us a hand. They spent the entire day boxing our belongings, hauling them out to a truck, carrying them into our new house, and unpacking them.

Afterward I met my new next-door neighbor. She was amazed to see how many people had come to help. I told her that everyone was from our church and that we believe in being involved in one another's lives. Her comment was, "That's what church ought to be like." Indeed, that's the church that will display the beauty of God's kingdom in a way that will draw the people of the world.

We have to guard against the attitude of independence that Vashti demonstrated. It's this attitude that says, "I don't need to be committed to other believers. I'm just dependent on the Lord." That may sound spiritual, but actually it expresses a self-centered mentality. Women with this outlook will go to endless trouble to be involved in some attractive ministry but are not available to be used in their own local church.

Someone can devise an ambitious plan to win their neighborhood for Christ, but putting it into practice without the prayer and cooperation of a church will be hard work. We need others to add their talents and share the burdens of ministry. New converts will grow quickly if their roots find the healthy soil of a loving, caring church, where they can be nourished and fed.

Let's pray for grace to recognize where we're functioning too independently, and then make adjustments. Let's be flexible and ready for change. Independence can manifest itself in an unwillingness to give up some work we've done successfully for years. Many a ministry has lost its effectiveness by being continued long after God's purpose for it has been accomplished. Years of energy can be poured into what is no longer God's best. It takes grace and humility to know when to stop.

INDEPENDENCE IN MARRIAGE

Vashti pitched in to do her part for the king's campaign to display the kingdom. She did fine outwardly until she refused to work in harmony with him. The moment she took things into her own hands by refusing Xerxes' command, she was no longer valuable in his campaign. Instead of promoting his kingdom she was promoting herself. That was her downfall.

Husbands and wives have a unique privilege: together they can demonstrate the harmony of a loving relationship. Vashti lost her opportunity because she was so wrapped up in her own concerns. God has called wives to support and encourage their husbands. This is a wife's first and most important ministry.

Some Christian couples operate in ministry like a two-career family. Each spouse has his or her own ministry and works independently. Everything might seem fine, but there is always a missing element. Scripture teaches that woman was created to be a companion and helper for her husband,[8] and to be alongside him to enhance his ministry. The two are to be one flesh, and that surely means a united ministry.

When a woman wholeheartedly embraces the privilege and responsibility of being a wife as a full-time commitment, she bestows "favor from the Lord"[9] upon her husband. Like the woman of noble character in Proverbs 31, she will "bring him good, not harm, all the days of her life."[10]

I know of one man who was adrift spiritually, while his wife, a frequent speaker, was forging ahead serving the Lord. Finally she decided to halt her speaking ministry and devote more time to being a wife and mother. During that time her husband grew in his faith, their marriage was strengthened, and her husband found his place in the church. Only when she began to put him first did he develop into a mature man of God. Later, she was able to resume her speaking engagements.

How thrilling it is when a woman chooses to sacrifice her own ministry involvement to give priority to being the wife her husband needs. Those who make this difficult decision always find that the joy of seeing a husband develop in his own sphere far outweighs the sacrifice.

Family and home life suffer if we allow our own particular ministry to loom too large among our spiritual goals. Beware of overshadowing your husband and discouraging him. Don't worry; God won't waste any of your gifts. He will use them in a richer way when you lay aside your independence. Working together always produces more fruit than working separately.

STUDY QUESTIONS
CHOSEN TO BELONG

1. We are all part of a worldwide family comprising all who belong to the body of Christ. God's plan for us is that we should enjoy tangible blessings from being in this family. Read 1 Corinthians 12 and discuss what it teaches about the local church.
   • Is there any Christian who can't belong?

- Should you belong?
- Is it possible to belong to the body of Christ but at the same time flit from church to church?
- Who is the most important member?
- Is there anyone who isn't needed?
- Have you found out what you can do to serve?

2. Read Colossians 3:12-14. How does it say we can all play our part in maintaining loving relationships in the family of God?

3. Pray that God would show you if you need to adjust your thinking or do something about belonging to a local church. Pray that you can find ways of serving the body of Christ.

5

FINDING YOUR PLACE

Once the queen's throne was vacant the men heaved a sigh of relief. Who would have thought a beautiful woman like Vashti would create such a crisis? Getting rid of Vashti didn't take long. Restoring the damage she had done would be much more demanding. Her rebellion was an example to the most influential women of the empire who, in turn, were examples to women everywhere. The authorities would have to tackle the matter carefully, or there would be no end to the dissension and turmoil.

To make sure everyone understood what was happening, messengers carried the news to every province. The queen was to be replaced by someone more worthy. But before this could happen, men would have to rule their households and women learn to respect their husbands. It was time to adjust their relationships. That would open the way for a new queen to reign. They were looking for a woman whose attitude needed no further adjustment.

This adjustment period is a perfect picture of what is taking place in God's kingdom today. Christian homes are experiencing a new harmony as husbands take their position as leaders and become the men God intended them to be. Wives are finding a new security and delight in submitting to husbands who rule lovingly over their families. Men are increasing in stature and expanding in ministry as they're encouraged by supportive wives. Many women are finding great relief in having the burden of total responsibility for certain areas taken off their shoulders.

Nonetheless, the adjustments have at times been painful. Working out in everyday life what it means to be free of Vashti-like independence takes time. Suddenly women find themselves facing deep inner struggles they never experienced when they operated independently.

Women who have worn the pants in the family have had to adopt a new way of life. Those accustomed to making snap decisions must learn to wait for someone else to make up his mind. Working women with responsible jobs might find that in ministry they have to defer to men who are not as well organized or as effective in administration.

We might falter at times. But we need patience and faith to draw upon the abundant grace God supplies. There is a throne to be occupied. Every small victory is a step toward entering a new dimension of freedom and authority.

Perhaps the women of Persia needed to make some adjustments. But it could well be that men needed to make some changes as well. The failure of men to rule their households opens the door for women to take over. Indeed, families can suffer greatly unless women fill the void. This pattern has been repeated throughout church history: when men fail to step forward, God uses women instead. But it's always with the better way in view.

Where would Israel have been without Deborah to inspire the men to rout the enemy? She led the nation, but was there no man for the job? Deborah gave Barak every opportunity to take the lead, but he lacked the courage to do it without her. [1] Despite this, Barak's name is among the heroes of faith listed in the eleventh chapter of Hebrews. Through Deborah's example, Barak became a hero of faith.

Trouble arises when modern Deborahs who have filled a leadership vacuum are unwilling to relinquish the reins when God's men come onto the scene. This requires grace and humility, but the reward is worth it. I know some lovely women, pioneers in ministry, who have done just that.

In Tanzania, a woman missionary served as director of a Bible school. She led young men to the Lord and discipled them, and they matured in the faith. Some went on to become pastors and responsible leaders. Years later, one of her male students came back and assumed her position at the Bible school. What was her response? "How wonderful," she said. "Praise the Lord!" What greater joy and reward could she have than to see men whom she had led to Christ assume leadership? If women refuse to release the reins, men will either diminish in stature or go elsewhere to lead.

Perhaps there was a period in Persia in which relationships were strained as men and women sought to comply with the new rules for their households. Four years passed with the queen's throne vacant. Maybe the king wasn't satisfied that everyone was obedient to his command that households come to order. The pressure was on to comply with the law.

Beware of bringing a similar pressure on yourself by adopting a legalistic attitude toward submission. The biblical principle of submission is designed to bring us into rest. God doesn't burden us with weighty rules to follow so we can be submissive women. Jesus, our example, *delighted* to do His Father's will. He didn't obey out of duty or obligation. Love was His motivation, and it should be ours.

> If you obey my commands, you will remain in my love,
> just as I have obeyed my Father's commands and remain
> in his love. I have told you this so that my joy may be in you
> and that your joy may be complete (John 15:10-11).

Submission that is not based on a loving relationship with God causes painful joints in the body of Christ. The lubricating fluid of love is missing.

If we submit with the wrong motivation it will be apparent. "I'll do what you say, but don't blame me when it proves to be a disastrous mistake." Or, "Okay, you make the decision, but I'm not going to live with any negative consequences." This isn't submission. It's blackmail. Men would rather work alone than cooperate with the cold "submission" of a disapproving woman. They would rather have a vacant throne.

King Xerxes had been in no hurry to find a new queen. But the pressure must have mounted as he grew lonely. Moreover, men likely took on tasks for which the queen had been responsible, and that undoubtedly became a burden. The sooner the king found the right wife to share the load the better. Only one woman in the empire would prove suitable. There in the city of Susa, God's woman was being prepared.

Church leaders today need women they can trust to carry out the ministry women do so well. Only a woman can be a queen. Just as a search began for someone to take Vashti's place, a search is now on for God's beautiful women, prepared and eager to serve, to fill the vacant throne. The Holy Spirit is putting into the hearts of God's men the desire to encourage women to fulfill their role. Are you available?

Some women are already taking their places of ministry in their local churches. For others, the opportunity has yet to come. I've heard some of their reactions to this situation:

"My leaders won't let me share some of the wonderful truths I've learned from God's Word."

"I know I could do that job better than some of the men. It's so frustrating."

Perhaps these would be your words if you verbalized your thoughts. One day you will have the opportunity to use your gifts. God won't waste them. Give Him your talents afresh to use whenever and however He wants. Often our abilities have to be like a kernel of wheat, which must first fall to the ground and die before it can spring up in fruitfulness.

Meanwhile, God has something for you to do. There are opportunities at hand where you can serve Him. In your job, in your family, whatever your daily work, that's where you can reign. That's where you can exert a godly influence. That's where you can be a queen.

Letting yourself gaze longingly into "forbidden territory" only brings discouragement. The land of "if onlys" is full of disappointment. Women of God need to go beyond these feelings to a point where their focus is on their present opportunities to serve. Whatever task comes your way, do it with all your heart, as unto the Lord. [2]

Before God opens the way for you to use your gifts, He wants to release you from frustration so you can freely enjoy your present role. Do you grumble and complain about your church? What do you do when things go wrong? Are you quick to blame your church leaders? Can they rely on you to be among those who will volunteer to help when it's needed? How did you respond the last time you were asked to do one of those "boring" jobs marked "For Women Only," knowing that your involvement would release men to do what you might consider to be more important tasks?

Those so-called boring jobs are God's means of testing our

suitability for other roles. When we respond with a ready heart, showing that we feel privileged to serve in any capacity, we are well on the way to occupying the throne. Nothing will make our leaders hesitate to entrust us with authority more than a wrong spirit. We need queens with humility, queens who can reign because they are totally submitted to the King.

We are living in a time of awakening. The church is coming alive. God's men are taking their rightful place, and women no longer need to bear the strain of doing men's work. We can look forward to finding a completely new place of authority. Like Queen Elizabeth, we can reign but not rule. We can exercise great influence for the kingdom without having the last word. Discard every hindrance and set your sights on that vacant throne. We shall see that God uses us to reign in any circumstance.

STUDY QUESTIONS
ATTITUDE

1. Esther 1:17-18 explains that Vashti's conduct produced a disrespectful attitude and disorder. God desires loving respect and harmony in the body of Christ. How can you do your part to please Him in this area?
2. Ephesians 5:21-24,33 indicates that submission is a key attitude. Is this something just for women? To whom does the call of submission apply?
3. To respect means to esteem and honor, to treat with deference. What does it mean to respect your husband? See Ephesians 5:33 and 1 Peter 3:7.
4. Read 1 Peter 3:1-6. How can wives live in harmony with their husbands?
5. Does submission imply inferiority? Was Jesus equal to the Father? See Philippians 2:6.
6. Philippians 2:3,4 shows that we need to get rid of wrong attitudes. What are they? What are the right attitudes? See Philippians 2:5-8.

6

ADVERSITY NO OBSTACLE

Excitement mounted as commissioners began to select queen candidates from among the empire's most beautiful young women. Influential families made sure their daughters were in view and looking their best. The long search touched every corner of the empire.

Where was the new queen? Who would have guessed she lived right in the capital city? Until then no one had noticed the orphan girl, Esther. Her name wasn't listed in the "Who's Who of the Persian Empire." She didn't move in the leading social circles. From a natural perspective, she was a nobody. But God had His hand on her.

The commissioners passed by thousands of other eligible young women to pick Esther as one of the queen candidates. What did this "nobody" have that the others lacked? It wasn't influential friends or a distinguished background. Esther had a disastrous start in life. Her people were taken captive and exiled from their homeland. Her parents had died, and she was dependent on the mercy of her cousin Mordecai. She was a stranger in a foreign land.

But this adversity had brought her to her destiny. Esther had no earthly father, but she had a heavenly Father who had a perfect plan in mind. The circumstances of her childhood proved no obstacle to her finding God's will. No matter what adversity comes our way, God will use it for good.[1] It's our reaction to hardship, not hardship itself, that can be a hindrance.

How easy it would have been for Esther to resent having been left parentless, exiled, and destitute. We aren't told how she lost her parents and the security and love of a family. But we do know that no festering self-pity, resentment, or bitterness marred her relationship with Mordecai, who took her in as his own daughter. Their relationship of mutual affection and esteem was to last a lifetime. Esther enjoyed showing her love for Mordecai by carrying out his wishes. She showed him honor and respect. How could she do otherwise after all his kindness to her?

Esther had a secure relationship with God and with her guardian. Poise and confidence are evident in a woman who is secure. These qualities set Esther apart. No wonder her attractiveness drew the attention of the king's commissioners. Those years of training in Mordecai's household had added a special ingredient to her beauty. Hers was not just outward attractiveness, but was also an inward beauty created by an attitude of respectful obedience. Esther won the favor of everyone who saw her.

God had chosen this queen even before she was born, and He had ordered her steps from the time she was in her mother's womb.[2] As she grew up in Mordecai's home, Esther had no idea of the future that lay before her. The challenges could have been daunting at an earlier age. But when God's moment came, she was ready.

Caught up in the vision of God's new and thrilling purpose for her life, Esther went willingly to the harem, the place of preparation for the queen candidates. Even though it meant leaving the security of Mordecai's house, she still felt safe. Mordecai gave her careful instructions, and she followed them as always. He visited her daily, checking on her welfare and offering assurance that he was close at hand.

The idea of a godly woman in a harem seems totally unacceptable. Surely the Lord could have found some other way to bring His chosen queen to the throne. Esther must have had misgivings about going into that heathen environment. But assured that God was with her, she was able to step confidently into the unknown. However trying the months ahead would be, she knew it would all serve as training for her future.

There is no better place to be than in the center of God's will. We may not understand why God allowed His child to be in a harem, but Esther knew it was God's will for her. Mordecai wouldn't have allowed it if he, too, had not understood God's plan for his beloved Esther. There is no need to shrink from any situation that looms before you. As long as you walk in submission to your heavenly Father, delighting to obey Him, you will find His will is absolutely perfect.[3]

Esther was ready to stride forward with God into a totally unexpected situation. Her attitude made all the difference. Esther could confidently join the other Persian women chosen for the harem, for she was certain she was fulfilling God's purpose. She was delighted at the prospect of becoming queen. She would do her best to make Mordecai proud.

God had gone before Esther. God had placed in charge a man who knew the difference between outward show and inward reality. He immediately recognized that here was a woman who was different, and he assigned her to the harem's most privileged place. This "nobody" was getting nothing but the best. Each day she was secure that God would provide her needs.

Esther was thrust into a completely different way of life. The following year was designed to find out whether she would be a suitable queen. She was given new responsibilities, including being put in charge of seven maids. Her ability to handle a measure of authority was being tested. The new queen would have to be someone who could be trusted with supervising the palace affairs.

The women of the harem were lavished with beauty aids. For twelve months they received every possible encouragement to develop their potential as beautiful women. No doubt Esther reveled in the rich perfumes, luxurious cosmetics, and special foods as much as anyone. It must have felt good to be served when she was used to serving others.

It was a busy, enjoyable life. Yet often her thoughts must have turned toward Mordecai and the home she'd left. Did she feel shut in? Did she ever long to get away? Was it frustrating to see Mordecai in the courtyard and not be able to invite him into the palace? When the routine and restrictions became irksome, what gave her peace of mind? It was the vision set before her: one day she would become queen.

We need to believe that God has chosen us to fulfill His purposes. Nothing in our lives has been a mistake. Failures come; opportunities are lost; but God uses them all as stepping stones to success. Constantly looking at the past blinds us from seeing where we're going. Like Esther, we're all in God's training program, learning valuable lessons that will serve a purpose later in our lives.

You may have caught a glimpse of how God plans to use you. Perhaps it stirs you with great excitement, but you see no immediate prospect of being freed from the restrictions of today's "chores" into the reality of your vision. A church leader's wife whom I know wanted to write Christian books, but she had a family with five small children. She waited, and in time the Lord provided people to come into her home and take care of her children so she could be released to write. She eventually became a successful author.

If you're in a situation like the one she was in, hold on! Recognize that God intends to use your present circumstances to build character that will allow you to fulfill His purposes. Let your attitude be transformed into one of faith and hope.

When I was a teenager, my great desire after graduating from high school was to go on to nurses' training. I had taken a special course to prepare myself. I felt sure this was God's plan for me. But instead of studying nursing I wound up doing clerical work in an office. It was deadly dull. I can remember gazing out the office window watching schoolgirls playing the sports I loved. I felt like a caged bird.

Then my parents moved to another city, and my hopes rose that I'd be able to begin training to become a nurse after all. World War II had begun, spurring a demand for nurses. With that, my possibilities brightened even more. At last I got an interview at the hospital that had the program I wanted. To my delight, I was accepted. But there was one hitch: I had to wait several months to start.

Once more it was back to the boring grind of my clerical job. I stuck it out and did my best, all the time longing for the day when I'd walk out of that office for the last time. One thing kept me going.

To get to work, I rode the train every day into the city. On one trip, I made an exciting discovery. As I stared out the window, the train passed an area where, for an instant, the hospital buildings came into view. They loomed tall on the horizon. Twice a day I gazed longingly at that sight, full of expectancy. That set me free to cope with the office routine.

Ask God to give you a vision for His purpose in your life. You have a destiny in God. You are to be a queen. Your circumstances are not an obstacle. They are God's assignments to prepare you, whether you realize it or not. Before you ascend to the throne you might have to endure a trying situation, as did Esther. Do what Abraham Lincoln did when he told himself as a young man, "I will study and get ready, and perhaps one day my time will come."

STUDY QUESTIONS
KNOW YOUR DESTINY

When Esther was called to the palace, her destiny was revealed. She set her sights on being chosen as queen and applied herself diligently to do God's will.

Every woman of God has a destiny. It requires our whole-hearted response.

1. Read Psalm 139:13-16. What does this passage have to say about how God has created us and shapes our destiny?
2. Read Ephesians 1:4-5 aloud. (The Living Bible translation is especially good: "Long ago, even before he made the world, God chose us to be his very own, through what God would do for us; he decided then to make us holy in his eyes, without a single fault — we who stand before him covered with his love. His unchanging plan has always been to adopt us into his own family by sending Jesus Christ to die for us. And he did this because he wanted to!")
   Why did God choose us? Did it have anything to do with our parents, our abilities, our appearance?
3. Read Ephesians 2:6. What privileged position do we share as believers?
4. Read Romans 5:17. What two gifts are available so we can reign triumphantly over life's circumstances?
5. Describe in practical terms what it means to reign, or to be queen, in God's kingdom. For help, read 1 Peter 2:9, Titus 2:3-14, and Ephesians 2:10.
6. Read Philippians 3:12-14. Paul gives us an example to follow. What is his attitude toward God's purpose for his life?

7

FROM PRISON TO PRIVILEGE

One can imagine a sentry posted outside the harem. His orders are to keep men out and women in. A sign at the door reads: "Women only! No men beyond this point."

Listen to the thoughts of a woman passing this secluded area: *Women only, eh? This place can't be as elaborate as the men's quarters. A man, of course, must be in charge. The women will have to do as they're told. How awful. No chance to please themselves. Think of being stuck with all those women. What a prison! How much better off men are.*

Some of us think of womanhood as this imaginary woman viewed the harem: something terribly restrictive. This is the product of negative thinking and low self-esteem so prevalent among today's women. We underestimate ourselves. We assume that a woman's role is inferior and her tasks only tedious. It's easy to forget that many men's jobs are monotonous and wearisome. Nor are men always free to please themselves.

We are in danger of being conned by Satan, the master of deception. He would convince us that we're unable to make full use of our gifts and unable to reach our potential. He would have us believe that because we're women we must accept a limited sphere of ministry. Satan wants to convince us that we're never free to initiate and that men have the most important tasks.

That's devilish nonsense. Yet godly women — with all their queenly authority and potential — fear stepping beyond this false concept of womanhood. Instead, they retire into their shells, afraid to use their gifts. This undermines faith and inhibits growth. When women who have retreated from ministry are given expanded opportunities, some of them have no desire to respond. When this happens everyone loses.

While some Christian women withdraw, others take a more belligerent stance, convinced they're victims of sexual discrimination. What can they do? It would be unspiritual to protest like the women of the world. So they just avoid any project designed only for women. Any suggestion that they support women's activities meets with no response. Unless men are involved they assume it must be second-rate.

How vital it is for us to throw off these shackles. God has chosen you for a special position that only a woman can occupy. By all means, let's stand up for our rights — the right to enjoy being a woman! Then we will enjoy real freedom.

Our society goes to great lengths to liberate women, yet these efforts only succeed in reinforcing the concept that women are imprisoned. The world has devised unisex clothes, unisex hairdressers, and carefully worded ads for unisex jobs. None of it alters the facts: women are women. To be a woman is not the misfortune of birth. It's a God-granted privilege.

The world's educational systems have been infiltrated by people campaigning in earnest for women's rights. In England, it's "discriminatory" for a school curriculum to contain compulsory cooking classes for girls. Girls must be free to study the same subjects as boys. Nobody would suggest that a technical course might be more appropriate for boys than for girls.

To some, this seems perfectly reasonable. But if anyone dares to voice the obvious — that girls are more likely to need cooking lessons than boys and that boys gravitate toward mechanical and technical trades — there is an outcry.

We need to be alert to recognize what lies at the root of this: an underlying belief that womanhood is restrictive, something from which women should be released. Some complaints of the women's liberation movement have been justified. Women have been exploited as a cheap labor force, for example. But such issues must not blind us to the false premise of the women's liberation movement that men and women must be equal in everything. In Christ, women and men have equality.[1] They are, however, different in function.

Esther turned the restrictions of the harem into the opportunity of a lifetime. Her mind was set on occupying that vacant throne, and she in no way regarded her womanhood as a limitation. As you anticipate exercising the authority of a queen, you can revel in being chosen to be a woman. The tasks already at hand — even our daily routines — should be seen as a test of our capabilities. God, who equips us with talents, expects us to use them.

Esther was assigned seven maids from among the palace servants. These women were experienced workers, accustomed to the routines of the royal household. How would Esther handle the responsibility of supervising them? They might try to manipulate the young newcomer: "Oh, no, Miss! We've always done it this way." But Esther's training in Mordecai's household stood her in good stead.

Esther learned to be gracious but firm. She would make sure everything was done thoroughly. Being faithful in the smallest details of household management was important preparation for queenship.

Esther certainly would have made good use of her seven maids. Not many of us are financially able to employ servants. Yet, in one sense, we all have "maids" to supervise. I have at least four faithful servants: my washing machine, clothes dryer, vacuum cleaner, and dishwasher.

You are responsible for managing your household equipment, from the simplest tools to the most complex appliances: dustmops and brooms, typewriters and tape recorders, televisions and videotape machines, calculators and cameras. A queen knows how to make the best use of her tools.

How well do you care for your "maids"? Do you bother to read the manufacturer's instructions? Do you overload the washing machine and then complain when it goes on the blink? Do you leave your barbecue grill out to rust in the rain? The foolish woman abuses her tools. The wise woman makes them last.

Christian women need to see their everyday household tasks — everything from tidying closets to planning meals and balancing the checkbook — as kingdom assignments. Being faithful in handling details qualifies us for greater responsibility.[2] A queen does things with excellence. Whatever the work, she does it with all her heart, for it's the Lord she's serving.[3]

Our path to the throne is paved with plenty of practical opportunities to develop our skills. Are you more proficient at your job than you were six months ago, or do you still make the same thoughtless mistakes? Does your boss know you'll work just as hard when he's gone as when he's there?

These are means of developing your character. Esther had something extra that impressed everyone around her. She was placed center stage, chosen for the best place in the harem. If she were careless, inattentive to detail, or moody, it would have been obvious to those around her. But her character stood the test.

Some of us might think, "It was fine for Esther to fiddle with all those details. She had seven maids. But how can I find the time?"

Esther probably faced a similar time crunch just trying to keep an eye on seven women. After sorting out priorities and planning the day's work for each of them, she probably had little time left for herself. It was no small assignment for Esther to manage her time well, and it's a challenge for most women today. In her excellent book, *How To Have All the Time You Need Every Day*, Pat King tells how she, the mother of a large family, discovered there is always enough time for the essential tasks. The Lord helped her order the priorities in her life. We need to make the same discovery.

A young woman unable to manage time poured out her problems to a friend of mine. She felt defeated, unable to accomplish much or to get anything done on time. Even her clock was unreliable, she moaned. My friend listened sympathetically. After giving her some spiritual encouragement, she parted with a word of advice: "Buy yourself a new clock."

Sometimes we can be waiting for some great spiritual revelation of how to cope when the solution may be obvious. Try making a list of all your possible tasks. When you're finished, pray that the Lord will show you which tasks He wants you to do and which you needn't worry about. Then ask God to show you how to rank your new list according to priority.

Spiritual growth cannot be divorced from practical responsibility. Esther's preparation involved daily chores and luxurious beauty treatments. The two went together as she matured in womanhood.

STUDY QUESTIONS
ENJOYING YOUR WOMANHOOD

1. Read Genesis 1:27. *Man* refers to both sexes in this passage. Both males and females are needed to reflect the true image and likeness of God. What is the woman's special contribution?
2. What commission were men and women to carry out together? See Genesis 1:26,28.
3. Psalm 46:1 and Psalm146:5 indicate that God is a helper. Certainly this is not an inferior responsibility but a privilege women can enjoy. Look up all the Scriptures you can find that describe the kind of help God provides. Psalm 28:7 is one example.
4. Galatians 3:28 says that in Christ we all have equal standing before God. Does this mean we all have the same function?
5. Women are commended in the Bible for their ministry. Look up the following Scriptures and list some tasks for which women are better suited than men: Matthew 27:55-56 and Acts 9:36-39. Can you think of any others?
6. Read Matthew 1:20-21. In order to fulfill His plan of salvation, God chose Mary to do what no man could do. What does this say about the value God has placed on women?

8

BORN-AGAIN BEAUTY

King Xerxes' harem became home for perhaps dozens of the most beautiful young women of the Persian Empire. These privileged women had to be gorgeous to be chosen. Then came twelve months of beauty treatments!

As Esther looked around at all the lovely forms and faces, she knew she couldn't rely simply on her natural good looks to set her apart. Something more was needed if she were to be the one to attract the king's attention.

The authorities were looking for a woman worthy of taking Vashti's place. Vashti, like all the women chosen for the harem, was strikingly beautiful. No one had seen the ugly traits in her character until it was too late. They didn't want to make the same mistake again, so they kept close watch on the candidates. With so many women living in close quarters and competing for the crown, it was an ideal situation to test their grace and character.

It must have been humbling for these women to discover that their beauty wasn't enough to satisfy the king. Moreover, they could use no cosmetics until a period of purification and cleansing was completed. During this first six months they applied the perfuming oil of myrrh. Today we have mud-pack facials. It seems that women of every era have subjected themselves to all types of strange rituals in the quest for beauty.

Whatever the ingredients, the basic process hasn't changed through the centuries. First cleansing, then beautifying. We don't just cover up the dirt. We clean our skin first, then apply make-up.

After months of purifying, the women's bodies took on the fragrance of perfume. No one could mistake the lovely aroma. Then the time came to apply cosmetics. For another six months nothing was spared as beauty experts labored over the queen candidates.

Throughout it all, Esther continued to win everyone's approval. She hadn't been spoiled by this intense, year-long effort focused on her appearance. Even though Hegai had given her the best place in the harem, she did not give way to the pride which could easily have brought her downfall. Esther exuded the same quiet humility that had first won her notice. While people worked on her outward appearance, God continued His work within.

If we had to depend on outward beauty to become queens in the kingdom, few of us would qualify. Even though we may nod our heads in agreement, some of us still have a sneaking suspicion that we would stand a better chance of becoming God's queens if we'd been born with certain talents or a different temperament. But here's the good news: you were not chosen because of your natural traits and abilities but in spite of them.

God in His love has chosen women of all shapes and kinds: the smart ones, the not-so-smart ones, the bustling ones, the slow ones, the flashy ones, the subdued ones. All the beauty necessary is given to us the moment we're saved. The ugly things of the past are gone; we're made new in Christ.[1] God, who looks on the heart, sees us as beautiful. We bring delight to His heart and are worthy of being displayed to the world. By His work, we're becoming more beautiful.

A beautifying process takes place for all those who aspire to be women of authority and influence in God's kingdom. Like the beauty treatments of the harem, this involves cleansing and purifying. Blemishes and weaknesses disappear, and the beauty of Christ is seen.

The cross has dealt with our ugliness. It is no longer I who live, but Christ who lives in me.[2] This basic work has been accomplished. But the Holy Spirit applies on us daily the oil of myrrh, which represents testing and suffering, so that the fruit of the Spirit might replace works of the flesh.

Like Esther, we might find ourselves in a crowd of women concerned only with themselves. Every time we allow a selfish, competitive spirit to motivate us, we feel the conviction of the Holy Spirit applying the myrrh. Once the purifying work is done and we can bring peace instead of strife, a lovely aroma fills the air.

Many women see no evidence of the beauty of Christ in their lives. Instead they see just the opposite as they battle some recurring sin. Out of their hearts comes the cry: "I so badly want the fruit of the Spirit to be seen in my life, but I seem to be so up-and-down. One day things are going fine, then the next, it's failure again. The same thoughtless word or deed."

Take heart. This sense of failure is all part of God's purifying process. He's never content just to paper over the cracks. It's always a step in the right direction when we realize we can't do it ourselves. We need divine resources. Jesus told His disciples to tarry until they were clothed with power from on high.[3] Every beautiful woman must know that only the Holy Spirit can give her the power and authority she needs to occupy the throne.

FITTING FOOD

Esther's beauty program also featured a healthy diet. I once read a book on natural foods titled *We Are What We Eat.* How true that is when it comes to spiritual nourishment. We grow spiritually according to how well we're fed.

For a healthy spiritual diet, it's not essential to go to Bible college or to shut yourself away for hours studying God's Word. Most of us, as much as we might like to, can't spare the time for either one. It's good to set aside a definite time regularly for prayer, Bible reading, and study. But we don't need hours on end. All we need is a healthy appetite and a good digestion! Women who want to ascend to the throne will be eager to receive every nourishing word they can get.

How's your appetite? God delights to fill those whose mouths are open wide. You might have lost your spiritual appetite because you're eating the wrong foods and feeding your mind with garbage. Don't waste time watching second-rate television programs or living in a magazine dream world. Cut out that kind of junk food in your diet, even if it means changing your lifestyle.

A little food well digested is better than gulping down a huge meal. This is also true in the spiritual realm. If we're to digest a spiritual truth, we have to chew it slowly and absorb it. This is the art of meditation. We don't have to wait until we're shipwrecked on a desert island to find the time. The busiest person can learn to hear from God and respond.

However full your life may be, you can still find five minutes to yourself, even if you have to shut yourself in the bathroom! In that short time, if you're hungry, God can draw your attention to a verse or phrase in His Word.

Begin to chew on it.

Repeat it.

Talk to God about it.

Think about it.

Write it down as soon as you can.

Chew on it through the day when you bring the verse to mind.

Pray for grace to do something about it.

You can help your digestion by memorizing the verse and by sharing it with someone else. You'll be amazed at the things God says to you as you meditate. When you respond by taking action on the truth, you can be confident your mind has begun absorbing spiritual nourishment. Joshua learned that meditation is the secret of success and prosperity.[4]

When you feel inadequate, wondering if you'll ever find victory, that's when you need a nourishing bite.

Do you lack faith and confidence? Why not start chewing right now? You were chosen long before you were born to be holy and blameless.[5] Yes, you! What's more, God undertakes the job Himself. He won't leave you struggling in defeat.[6]

God puts us through the purifying process because He loves us, because He wants a people who are "His very own, eager to do what is good."[7] His dealings are always perfectly timed and perfectly suited to each individual. Purifying often involves discipline and chastening. Though unpleasant at the time, these dealings of God are tremendously worthwhile, bringing peace and righteousness.[8]

Some years ago I longed to have more power in my life. I wanted to be more effective, to be set on fire for God. I prayed in earnest, "Lord, baptize me with fire." The answer was unexpected and humiliating. Instead of being raised into glory on the mountain top I found myself in the thick fog of the valley. I had plenty of time to pray, but the heavens seemed like brass.

Soon I could almost feel the Holy Spirit burning within me, painfully convicting me of things deep within my conscience that had never been thoroughly dealt with. As a young Christian I had sinned and been too proud to confess my failure openly. By my own efforts I had papered over the cracks. But now in answer to my prayer the purifying process had begun.

The Holy Spirit is always specific in His dealings with us. He does not give us a vague feeling of condemnation from which there is no escape. I knew exactly what He was pointing out. As I acknowledged it and humbled myself by sharing it with my husband, immediately the fog lifted.

However God chooses to purify us and enhance our beauty, the result is always a new joy and sense of freedom. There's nothing like a clear conscience to add light to the eyes and radiance to the expression. That kind of beauty is essential for a queen.

STUDY QUESTIONS
HEALTHY EATING HABITS

God doesn't want us to go on a crash diet spiritually. He's more concerned that we develop healthy habits that produce lasting fruit.

1. How did God feed His people in the wilderness? See John 6:31.
2. How does God feed us? See John 6:33-35.
3. Read Exodus 16:4-30. What lessons can we learn from the Old Testament story about the Israelites, knowing we're not under the law but under grace? God gave them strict rules concerning their daily food. It was ideally suited to their situation. God likewise has a perfect plan for each of us. Do you follow a plan for feeding on God's Word, or are you careless and haphazard?
4. What happened when the Israelites didn't follow God's plan? See Exodus 16:20, 27. What can we learn from that?
5. One day each week the Israelites gathered no manna. If at times

you are unable to find time to read the Bible, will you lose out?

6. How else can you feed on the "bread of life" besides reading it? (One example is by singing Scripture songs.)

7. Read Joshua 1:8. This teaches us to cultivate the habit of meditation, taking time to ponder and pray about what God says to us. This can only be developed when we feed regularly on God's Word. What benefits come from meditation? See Psalm 1:3.

9

A NEW LOOK

"Will it be me?"

The question resounded in the mind of every woman in the harem. Esther had won Hegai's approval. Would she also win the king's? If only she could find out what would please him!

The time came at last for the women to be presented to the king. Each one could choose anything she desired to bring with her. It would be the first chance to make an impression. Should Esther bring a gift — a jeweled ring, a fine tapestry, a burnished sword, a prize steed?

And what to wear? Which gown? Which jewelry? Which hairstyle?

Imagine the anguish of making these decisions. So much was at stake. Once a woman left the harem, there was no turning back.

Unlike others, Esther didn't spend long debating what to bring and what to wear. Her humility paved the way for a quick decision and saved her much anxiety and tension. She simply asked Hegai to make the choices for her. How wise. No one knew the king's preferences better than Hegai.

She strode out confidently to meet the king, knowing she had done all she could to be pleasing to him. Many women dread the thought of arriving at an important event and discovering they're dressed unsuitably. Esther had no reason to worry. The God who had brought her to this place was with her. Her confidence was in Him.

This was the moment for which she'd prepared over those long months. Much more than she even knew hinged on this crucial encounter. Esther had come to the crossroads of history. Her training in character, her joyful obedience, and her deep sense of purpose would propel her toward her destiny in God.

We're given no record of this first encounter between Esther and the king. But we do know that he found Esther to be a delight. His heart was drawn to her more than to any other. He had no doubt. She was to be the new queen.

Esther succeeded because she took her cue from Hegai, following his every suggestion on her apparel. It's easy for us to learn what adorning will please our heavenly King. Scripture makes it clear that the beauty He values comes not from lovely clothing and attractive make-up. More than anything, He desires an inner beauty that nonetheless shows itself on the outside. Scripture says the unfading beauty of a gentle and quiet spirit is of great worth in God's sight.[1] It's seen in our behavior, our speech, and especially in our relationships.

Some women might think: "That's great for the lucky ones born with a nice, subdued temperament. But when I try to keep quiet and repress my natural exuberance, it isn't long before I burst!"

If you can identify with that, I have good news for you. A meek and quiet spirit has nothing to do with personality. That soft-spoken woman who always seems even-tempered may be holding down a volcano inside.

A gentle and quiet spirit isn't a function of your personality; it has to do with who is in control. Is it you or Jesus? When He is chief in your life, then your actions and reactions are also under His control. You won't present sweet smiles on the outside when at the same time you're full of tension within. With Jesus in charge, there will be genuine patience, freedom from hasty reactions, gentleness, and loving consideration.

I once asked a friend, "What do you think of when you hear the words 'a meek and quiet spirit'?"

"Oh," she said with a sigh. "All I know is that I haven't got it." We talked awhile about these qualities and agreed we had never met a woman who dared claim she had them. Should we all be so modest, or is this concept of an unattainable meek and quiet spirit another of Satan's tactics to convince us we'll never make it?

The Bible assures us that if any woman is in Christ, she is a new creation.[2] *In Christ* describes how God sees us right now. Likewise, Scripture says that all who have been baptized into Christ have clothed themselves with Christ.[3]

Surely this clothing includes the lovely spirit of meekness. Jesus described Himself as gentle and lowly of heart.[4] These Scriptures challenge us to repent of our unbelief and begin to behave like the beautiful women God has made us to be.

Esther's array of cosmetics and perfumes were ingredients that prepared her for what lay ahead. The beauty formula we need doesn't come in jars, but in the Scriptures. Through the precious promises of the Bible we have everything we need for life and godliness, everything we need to become like Christ.[5] We must put on these qualities by faith.

You can't take a jar of meekness from the shelf and rub it on yourself before beginning each day. But you can submit yourself afresh to Jesus and say, "Lord, You be in control. I delight to do Your will." That's how, through faith, you can put on Christ.[6] That's how you can know you've chosen the right perfume, the fragrance that pleases your heavenly Father.[7]

When we step out in faith like that, things happen. We suddenly become more aware of the areas in our lives where we need to apply the beautiful promises of Scripture. Life goes on with the usual frustrations — a husband is grumpy, a boss is unreasonable, the children squabble, a hurtful letter arrives in the mail — but we are not the same.

Instead of wanting to escape to some peaceful place, we hear a voice saying, "Take my yoke upon you and learn from me, for I am gentle and humble in heart, and you will find rest for your souls."[8] It's just as if Jesus offers to walk beside us into each situation, linking us to Himself by His yoke. That's putting on Christ. It requires a conscious act of submission and faith.

I had to learn this during the extremely trying years I cared for my elderly mother-in-law, whose mind had failed. I felt imprisoned by circumstances beyond my control and was desperate to escape the constant restrictions. My patience dried up completely.

The most difficult thing was giving up my own rights. As long as this needy woman was in our home, our lifestyle centered on her.

Our privacy was invaded. A battle raged within my spirit as I longed to be free. Other relatives shared the responsibility, so there were times of respite. But that didn't remove the burden or answer the question, "Lord, how long will this go on?"

I couldn't even fully enjoy the relief periods. I was weighed down with the dread of knowing I would have to cope with the situation once again in a few days. I was looking for freedom through escape, but God wanted me to find freedom in the situation. This liberation began the moment I recognized that my all-wise, all-loving heavenly Father was in control. He was using these circumstances as part of a beauty therapy I hadn't realized I needed. I was able to say, "Okay, Lord. I'll hand over my rights and delight to do Your will."

The situation didn't change. But I did. In that act of submission I had accepted the yoke of Christ, and I could face the trial with a new peace. I found that I could enjoy the brief respites like never before.

Still, it wasn't all smooth sailing. Each day brought new lessons to learn. I had to learn to put on the right adorning for each challenge. I had to cope with the myriad difficulties presented by dealing with my mother-in-law's failed mind, such as being willing to patiently answer the same question again and again.

In Jesus' beauty school, the supplies of fresh adorning are never exhausted. The fact that we don't always succeed in our efforts to put them on does not disqualify us. Our heavenly Teacher encourages us in our successes and keeps reminding us of the grace available in times of need. He has a marvelous wardrobe for us. He would have us arrayed in compassion, gentleness, patience, kindness, courtesy, courage, wisdom, humility, peace, love, faithfulness, and perseverance.

Putting on Christ means putting off self, and that means being willing to change. Dare to believe that God means what He says: "*It is God who works in you* to will and to act according to his good purpose."9 God is eager to array in splendor all who are willing. He wants to enjoy the beauty He has given you and let others enjoy it too. Your children, friends, and relatives will all reap the benefit.

Satan tries to make sure your mistakes loom so large that you fail to recognize the changes that have taken place. Your family probably won't tell you they appreciate your meek and quiet spirit.

They'll just enjoy having a mom who doesn't nag or a sister who isn't cross anymore. Your husband may never express his appreciation for what you do for him. But when you continue doing just the same, without grumbling, that's real progress.

People may not praise you, but inside you'll feel a wonderful new rest. The striving will cease and the burden will become light, just like Jesus promised. We know He sees us, and that's what really counts. Like Esther, we can be confident we're clothed aright. When our big moment comes we won't be afraid. We'll be ready to be used in every way to make the gospel attractive.[10]

Does all this mean that you should stop wearing nice clothes or bothering about your outward appearance so you can develop inner beauty? No, Scripture doesn't say that. It simply points out that what is most important in God's eyes is what we look like inside. Expensive clothes won't change us, but neither will hand-me-downs.

But once you're changed on the inside, it's bound to have an influence on the clothes you choose to wear and the way you care for your appearance. Your clothes will all bear a new label: "For His glory." That surely means taking the trouble to be clean, neat, and attractive and looking like you enjoy being a woman. Purity and modesty, however, will be of more concern than the latest fashion.

Esther's beauty was not the easily fading, superficial variety. Time only added to her splendor. The more the king saw of Esther, the more she won his heart. Her character dispelled any fears that another Vashti would emerge.

Don't listen to the negative accusations of the enemy who opposes you taking your place as a queen. Enjoy your beauty treatment, confident you are winning the approval of the King of Kings.

STUDY QUESTIONS
WHAT TO WEAR?

1. We're free to pick out the clothes we like. Are we also responsible for choosing how we will clothe our inner spirit?
   What types of clothing are discussed in Romans 13:14; Ephesians 4:22-24; and Colossians 3:12? Are we commanded

to wear these garments, or are they just optional accessories?

2. Can you find similar verses? A concordance will help.

3. What will make it possible for you to obey these commands? See 2 Thessalonians 1:11; Hebrews 11:6; and 2 Corinthians 5:7.

4. What's the basis of our confidence? See Philippians 2:12-13 and 1 Thessalonians 5:23-24.

5. Why do we get discouraged in our efforts to obey God? See Revelation 12:10.

6. How can we master sin and failure? Read Romans 6:14,16,22 and Romans 8:1-2.

7. What powerful influence is at work within us to overcome our weaknesses? See Titus 2:11-13.

10
TAKING THE THRONE

At last, the great day had come when the king placed a crown upon Esther's head. All eyes were on the king's beautiful new bride. In her honor, the king held a banquet with a long list of distinguished guests. There was no television to broadcast the ceremony and celebration, but the guests would soon go home and begin scattering details of the event across the empire.

An unknown orphan girl had ascended to the throne. She had come without important connections, without putting on a big show. Esther had risen from nowhere and won the hearts of the nation. She was truly God's chosen woman. King Xerxes was convinced this woman was worthy of honor. From that day forward, things were never the same. She was now Queen Esther. Someone to be respected. Royalty.

BORN TO BE A QUEEN

We, as Christians, have also been raised to a high position. God has put within us His most precious treasure, the life of Christ. We are of great value and use to God. Many women have difficulty believing this and struggle to accept themselves as God has made them. We don't need tremendous skills and talents to exercise authority in the kingdom. We need to be reminded again and again that He has chosen the weak, the foolish, the nobodies of the world, so that no one can boast before Him. "We have this treasure in jars of clay," Scripture says, "to show that this all-surpassing power is from God and not from us."[1] Our authority is His all-surpassing power.

You can take the throne right now just as you are. You don't

65

have to have your life totally together. You don't have to have any outstanding abilities. Having the beauty of Christ in your life is all you need to wear the crown. If you've been born again, you qualify.

There came a day in the life of England's Queen Elizabeth when, as a nine-year-old girl, she realized that she would be queen. From the moment she understood she was to be a queen, her life was no longer the same. Neither will yours be when you fully comprehend your new identity in Christ. You are called and chosen of God. Absorb down in your bones the truth that God has a plan for you. He plans to use you for His kingdom, and His plan is totally within your reach.

The revelation that you have been chosen as God's woman won't come by looking at yourself. It will come from God's Word. Sometimes we need to repeatedly review the Scriptures before a revelation sinks into our hearts. Consider these:

- "For he chose us in him before the creation of the world to be holy and blameless in his sight" (Ephesians 1:4).
- "In him we were also chosen, having been predestined according to the plan of him who works out everything in conformity with the purpose of his will . . . for the praise of his glory" (Ephesians 1:11-12).

When these Scriptures are made real to you, it will be like putting on heavenly eyeglasses. Your self-image and your attitude about your daily tasks will be transformed. You don't become a queen by having important tasks. Your tasks are important because you are a queen. God is at work in you, and He wants you to radiate His glory. Whether you're at home or on a job, God has an excellence for you to demonstrate. He's going to use you for His royal business.

Esther was confident of her true identity in God. We're not told that Esther was physically more beautiful than the other women. It was the manner and bearing of a godly woman that set her apart.

A QUEEN WORTHY OF RESPECT

Influential women in God's kingdom are, like Paul says of deacons' wives, women worthy of respect.[2] Their behavior demonstrates character that is worth copying. Charm is deceptive, Scripture says, and beauty is fleeting. But a woman who fears the Lord is to be praised.[3] Solomon paints a vivid description in Proverbs 31 of this kind of woman.

> She gets up while it is still dark; she provides food for her family and portions for her servant girls. She considers a field and buys it; out of her earnings she plants a vineyard. She sets about her work vigorously; her arms are strong for her tasks. She sees that her trading is profitable . . . . She opens her arms to the poor and extends her hands to the needy.[4]

The fear of the Lord is the secret of her many accomplishments. A woman who fears the Lord hates evil[5] and is God-centered. Like David, she can say: "I have set the Lord always before me. Because he is at my right hand, I will not be shaken."[6] Her aim is to love God with an undivided heart, and everything she does bears a royal stamp: "God's woman at work."

Suddenly Esther had to become accustomed to being treated as the queen. But with this came the responsibility she couldn't escape: she had to act like the queen she was. Everyone knew she was the first lady. Whatever she did became a royal occasion. There were royal decisions, royal menus, royal clothes, royal rooms.

Through it all, Esther demonstrated the nobility of character of which Solomon spoke. He also said this of the noble woman of God: "Her husband has full confidence in her and lacks nothing of value. She brings him good, not harm, all the days of her life."[7] It would not be long before King Xerxes reaped this benefit in a most dramatic way.

Esther settled into the palace and became occupied with affairs of state. But still she kept close ties with Mordecai. He often sat at the king's gate, a local gathering place and a heavily traveled entry point. Royal guards and officials were stationed there. One day Mordecai overheard a conversation between two royal officials who were devising a plot to assassinate King Xerxes. Mordecai quickly sent a warning to Esther. She, in turn, informed the king, giving the credit to Mordecai. The plot was foiled and the king's life spared.

NO JOB TOO SMALL

Esther had only acted as a messenger. Yet the way she performed the task would later be used in God's marvelous plan. The story of Mordecai's loyalty was entered in the book of records, and that later proved crucial in rescuing God's people from destruction.

Faithfulness in details qualifies us to be trusted with greater responsibility. Many women spend much time, either at home or work, answering the telephone, handling information, and being a relay link in the chain of communication for those they serve. The way we handle these assignments can convey lasting impressions. The reputation of our employer can hinge on the quality of our communication. A "queen" will be gracious and utterly reliable; she won't forget vital details. Whatever the task, she is clothed with strength and dignity.[8] It's all part of promoting God's kingdom.

We can mistakenly assume that being a woman of authority means assuming some prominent position of ministry. On the contrary, we might find ourselves like Esther, spending most of our time quietly reigning in the background. Keeping in touch with Mordecai, however, enabled her to be ready when the need arose. No job is too insignificant when it has that stamp of divine authority upon it.

THE PROMISE OF POWER

Esther was growing in confidence. Officials and servants alike recognized her authority as she quietly carried out the king's wishes. Her new relationship with the king had given her the power she needed to function.

By obeying our King's commands and walking in His ways, we can know His power. Jesus told His disciples that He had all power and authority in heaven and on earth.[9] Then He commanded them to wait until they were clothed with the same power.[10] It's essential equipment for a queen.

Jesus wants us to learn how to exercise the authority of His throne. That's the only way we can function effectively in His kingdom. He sent His Holy Spirit to equip us with all the power we need. Peter told a crowd in Jerusalem: "You will receive the gift of the Holy Spirit. The promise is for you and . . . for all whom the Lord our God will call."[11] These words, spoken on the day of Pentecost, should be embraced by every woman in Christ.

The Holy Spirit is given as a royal seal marking us as living "to the praise of his glory." [12] Like Mordecai, the Spirit is a comforter and counselor.[13] Through Him our relationship with Jesus comes alive. He makes known to us what Jesus is saying through His word.[14] The Holy Spirit also helps us in our weakness[15] and gives us assurance that our prayers are reaching the throne.

Esther would have floundered in a time of crisis if she hadn't continued her steady communication with Mordecai during periods of routine. Likewise, when carrying out seemingly insignificant chores, we need the Holy Spirit just as much as when we're doing something spectacular. Then we won't be caught unawares when opportunity comes. We'll be in tune with God and ready to move in faith.

To receive the power of the Holy Spirit, we need only ask. Noting that sinful earthly parents know how to give good gifts to their children, Jesus said, ". . . how much more will our heavenly Father give the Holy Spirit to those who ask him!"[16]

The Holy Spirit comes upon us in ways perfectly suited to each individual. For some, it's a dramatic and noisy occasion, as on the day of Pentecost. For others, the Spirit comes as quietly as refreshing dew. But one thing is common to all who receive the Holy Spirit baptism: assurance that He has come.

Esther continued her reign, going about her daily duties. She was unaware of the mounting tension at the palace gates. A crisis was soon to break upon her. But it would not find her unprepared.

STUDY QUESTIONS
FEARING GOD

1. Proverbs 31:30 highlights the key to success for a queen in God's kingdom. "Charm is deceptive, and beauty is fleeting; but a woman who fears the Lord is to be praised." Search for several Scripture references to the "fear of the Lord." What does it mean to you to fear the Lord? What kind of attitude does it involve?

2. Psalm 34:11 explains where we learn the fear of the Lord. What are some of the first lessons? See Psalm 34:13-14.

3. Read and discuss Psalm 25:14. (Look at the translation in the

New International Version or The Living Bible.) What is God's relationship with those who fear Him?

4. How will this affect your understanding of God's will? See Psalm 25:12.

5. Will this increase your understanding and knowledge of God's ways? See Isaiah 33:5-6.

6. Will the fear of the Lord affect your other fears and insecurities? See Psalm 112:1,6-8.

7. How should it affect church life? See Acts 9:31.

8. How can you learn the fear of the Lord more quickly? See Proverbs 2:1-5.

9. What's the key to understanding the fear of the Lord? Is this something you must grasp intellectually? See Proverbs 2:10 and Proverbs 18:15.

11

PUT TO THE TEST

Palace security was tightened after the discovery of the assassination plot. It was virtually impossible to approach the king without a personal invitation. Woe to anyone who dared disobey the rules. Haman the Agagite had been chosen to keep a tight grip on the king's affairs. He was Xerxes' proud and powerful chief official. Everyone was expected to pay him homage and kneel as he passed.

For Mordecai, this posed a dilemma. Haman was a descendant of Agag, king of the Amalekites. God had said He would erase the memory of the Amalekites from the earth because they had fought the Israelites.[1] How could Mordecai, a Jew, bow down before a man whose nation God had ordered to be destroyed? Should he dodge the issue by scurrying away whenever Haman passed by? That could limit his access to the queen, and Esther needed him all the more with such a wicked man influencing her husband.

Mordecai was not one to compromise. He resolved not to avoid Haman. Neither would he avoid the king's gate, where the many royal officials would notice Mordecai's actions. It was no small decision. His life was at stake.

At the king's gate, Mordecai had made no secret that he was a Jew, and the royal officials stationed there resented him. Orders had been given for everyone to bow to Haman, and whole crowds on the streets of Susa knelt as he passed. This foreigner had exempted himself from the king's command and was getting away with it. They repeatedly scolded him, but Mordecai stood firm. Finally, the officials told Haman about Mordecai. He was furious.

We may not face such serious consequences with our choices, but many issues arise in our daily lives that tempt us to compromise.

It's always possible to take an easy way out, to follow the crowd, knowing what's going on is wrong. But sticking to our convictions in small matters flexes our spiritual muscles and strengthens us for times of open conflict with the enemy. As women of God, let's be scrupulously honest. Let's be willing to suffer persecution for Christ's sake. Let's determine to remain pure in the midst of an immoral society.

As a young Christian, I worked in an office where I faced one of these minor issues of conscience. When employees came in to work each day, they all wrote down their names and the time they arrived on a single time sheet. You were in for trouble with the boss if you showed up late. One morning I missed my train into the city and arrived after starting time. I wanted to be honest about it. But I knew of others who regularly came in late and weren't so scrupulous. Because everyone who came in after me would write their names below mine, they'd all be forced to register their late arrival. I logged my true arrival time and paid a price for it. I wasn't too popular.

Once Haman learned there was a Jew who refused to pay him homage, Haman determined he would have every Jew in Persia killed. Mordecai had played into his hands. Here was an ideal opportunity for Haman to wreak vengeance on the nation he hated. These were the people who had destroyed so many of his ancestors.

Haman had someone cast lots to determine a lucky date for annihilating the Jews. The lot fell on a day nearly twelve months ahead. God had begun intervening even at that early hour! Much would take place during the coming months.

Haman used his persuasive powers to convince the king that all Jews were traitors, lawbreakers, and a bad influence on the nation. He urged the king to wipe them out once and for all and offered him a huge sum — 10,000 silver talents — to get the job done. The king declined the money, but nevertheless agreed to have the Jews destroyed. Haman's orders were written in the king's name and sealed with his ring. All Jews — men, women, and children — were to be killed and their goods plundered. It seemed as if the enemy had triumphed and God's people were doomed.

Mordecai was grief-stricken at this devastating turn of events. Inside the palace, the highly favored Haman was unassailable.

Mordecai tore his clothes, put on sackcloth and ashes, and cried loudly and bitterly in the city square for the Jewish people. When Jews across the empire heard of Haman's plan, they were terrified. The people mourned, fasted, and prayed earnestly that their God might spare them.

Esther was distressed when her servants told her they saw Mordecai, dressed in sackcloth, wailing outside the palace gates. Her immediate reaction was to try to relieve Mordecai's suffering by sending out good clothes for him. Her gesture said, in effect, "I'll take care of you. Now that I'm queen, you can come under my protection."

But this natural protective instinct would not have accomplished God's purposes. The Lord had a better way. Mordecai refused the clothes and restrained Esther from a hasty emotional response. Women can easily make the mistake of jumping in too quickly to protect loved ones from trials rather than first finding out what God has in mind.

My son and his wife recently went through a very difficult time. They had launched out in faith to start a new business that would serve the interests of the kingdom. But the pressures mounted as one difficulty followed another. How I longed to do something! My prayers concentrated on asking God to remove the obstacles — quickly. But God's way of love was better than mine. When the pressure finally let up, they had this testimony: "This was the most difficult year we've ever had, but we wouldn't have missed it for anything. God has taught us so much." If I'd had my way, I'd have robbed them of a blessing.

Back at the palace, Esther instructed her servants to find out exactly what Mordecai's distress was about. Mordecai made sure nothing was omitted in his report, including a copy of the order decreeing their destruction. He was not the only one who needed help; the Jewish nation's existence was at stake.

Replacing Mordecai's mourning clothes wouldn't meet the need. The most important thing Esther could do was obtain the king's help. She would have to use her influence to gain an audience with him and plead for mercy.

Mordecai had warned Esther of the mistake of using her position to act on impulse. Of course it was right to alleviate her cousin's distress. Of course it was right to do something for her people. But it wasn't yet time to identify herself with those who had been denounced as lawbreakers. She might incur her husband's wrath.

This was Esther's big challenge: learning to use her authority properly. Authority had been given her for a purpose beyond anything she had imagined. The key to using it correctly lay in the principle of submitting to God and to those over her. As queen, she could no more save her people by acting independently than she could as an unknown orphan.

Mordecai sent an urgent message to Esther requesting that she go before the king. She replied by explaining that going unbidden into the king's presence would mean certain death unless the king spared her by holding out a golden scepter. How could she be so certain of the king's love for her?

It had been thirty days since the king had sent for Esther. But there was no time to wait until the king might ask to see her again. Mordecai urged her to take her life into her hands, trusting she would be accepted by the king. He had some sobering words: "If you remain silent at this time, relief and deliverance for the Jews will arise from another place, but you and your father's family will perish." Then he gave her something else to think about: "Who knows but that you have come to royal position for such a time as this?"[2]

Esther did have an appointment with destiny. But she had never faced such a challenge. It was one thing to exercise a queen's authority in the daily palace affairs, but quite another to risk her life.

The powerful Haman had succeeded in obtaining the king's blessing on his plan to wipe out the Jews. How could she, a woman, oppose him and win? No man in the entire empire had so much influence. The odds seemed hopeless. But in faith she agreed to go. It was indeed God's plan to use this young queen as she learned to wield her authority.

Like Esther, we have to learn to control our natural emotions. Then the Holy Spirit can check us from hasty action. But he can also prompt us to attempt something even though we feel utterly inadequate. Fear can only be overcome by the assurance that we're acting in God's will. Our obedience has far-reaching consequences. Who knows what great purposes for our lives have yet to be revealed?

STUDY QUESTIONS
READY FOR THE UNEXPECTED

A woman who is God-centered is ready to cope with whatever comes her way. Let's look at how to respond to situations that often come up unexpectedly.

1. **Temptations to compromise.** Read 1 John 1:5-6; Ephesians 5:8-11; and Matthew 5:14-16. How do these verses teach us, like Mordecai, not to compromise when temptations arise?
2. **Questions and opposition.** How do we handle situations when someone is questioning our faith? See 1 Peter 3:13-16.
3. **Handling your reactions and emotions.** Emotions affect your behavior. What are some biblical guidelines for dealing with emotions such as anger? Start by looking at Ephesians 4:26-27; Proverbs 16:32; James 1:19; and Galatians 5:22-25.
4. **Tests of courage.** How can we become like Esther, who overcame her natural fear and found courage to obey Mordecai's request? See Isaiah 12:2; Psalm 34:4; and Philippians 4:4-7.
5. **Looming problems.** When problems seem like mountains, Psalm16:7-8 helps us see them in proper perspective. Psalm 37:5 tells us what to do. Psalm 145, which describes God's character, offers encouragement.
6. **Adversity.** When adversity strikes, who is in control? See Romans 8:28-39.

12

THE QUEEN IN CRISIS

Esther weighed the facts. She considered the risks. The decision was made.

"I'll go to the king," she said. "If I die, I die."

Brave words. But this time her decision wasn't just an emotional impulse. Now she understood why God had chosen her to be queen at this hour, and she was willing to risk her life to do His will.

She realized impatience could be a fatal flaw. Instead of impulsiveness, Esther showed a quiet trust. She found strength as she heeded Mordecai's counsel to do only as God directed. As queen, she could have safely distanced herself from the dangerous turmoil. But instead God called her to deny herself and lay down any such privilege.

God was not asking her to foolishly throw her life away, rather to simply and calmly obey. Jesus said, "If anyone would come after me, he must deny himself and take up his cross daily and follow me. For whoever wants to save his life will lose it, but whoever loses his life for me will save it."[1] That's the challenge facing every woman who desires to be influential in Christ's kingdom.

There is no authority, Scripture says, except that which God has established.[2] Hence, like Esther, we need to display our faith in God's established order by obeying those over us. However, if they require us to do something contrary to the will of God, then we have no choice but to obey God rather than men.[3]

King Xerxes, though unaware of the implications, had been persuaded to identify himself with God's enemies. If Esther were to appeal to him for a change of plans, she would need to tread carefully. This was too complicated a matter to be worked out by human wisdom. She would make only one move: pray for guidance. Even though the situation was urgent, her top priority was taking time to seek the Lord. Without hesitation, Esther gave Mordecai her instructions: "Gather together all the Jews who are in Susa, and fast for me. Do not eat or drink for three days, night or day. I and my maids will fast as you do."[4]

Instead of acting alone, Esther gathered the prayer support of the Jews outside the palace as well as her own prayer group inside. Esther's confidence that her maids would join her in prayer indicates that she had probably taught them to pray and that they had prayed together previously. Even while living in the luxury of the palace, Esther had not been ashamed or too busy to maintain her devotional life.

This was her key to success. Before petitioning the king, she knew she must first petition the King of Kings. What could a woman do to undermine the power of Haman? She would call upon her God, the Almighty who promises to give wisdom to all who ask.

If a crisis were to hit your life, would you be caught unawares? Have you learned to discipline your body, to set aside times of fasting and prayer? Jesus said," *When* you fast . . ."[5] not *"If* you fast . . . ." He expects His disciples to seek Him in this way.

We can fast by skipping just a single meal or by going without food for several days. But fasting has no virtue unless our motives are God-centered. When we fast because of the Holy Spirit's prompting, it has great value. In fasting we declare to God and to spiritual forces in high places that we are in earnest. We declare our determination to be part of that glorious church that will triumph over all the powers of darkness and pave the way for Christ's return. It will be a fasting and praying church that will hear the cry, "Behold the Bridegroom."[6]

Three days was long to wait when so much was at stake, but Esther was following God's timetable. Later events made this clear. So much hinged on exact timing. Guided by the fear of the Lord, Esther was patient and self-controlled. On the third day she knew with confidence what she must do. God's moment had come.

Esther hadn't received any thundering revelation. She just felt an assurance that it was time to speak to the king. She felt directed to invite him to a banquet, and to do something she couldn't have anticipated: invite Haman as well!

Had she really heard this from God? Wouldn't it be best to speak to the king alone? Perhaps Esther raised these questions in her mind. But whatever God said, she determined to do it. Esther donned her most splendid royal outfit, then strode out to her divine appointment in the inner court.

As she passed by palace guards and royal officials, they must have stared in disbelief, groping for an explanation. Then she walked into the court. There she stood: a woman who dared enter the forbidden place. Others, no doubt, had been executed for being so bold.

By faith, Esther was declaring to the king and to all onlookers that she had a right to enter. Everyone's gaze was fixed on King Xerxes. Would he be angry? By doing nothing, keeping his scepter at his side, he could condemn the queen to death for her trespass.

Then in one breathless moment, King Xerxes extended his scepter. He was delighted to see her and eager to know what she wanted so badly that she would risk her life. Before Esther said a word, the king asked, "What is it, Queen Esther? What is your request? Even up to half the kingdom, it will be given you."[7] King Xerxes was underlining her authority and expressing his trust in her.

All the officials wanted to know her request. But their curiosity would not be so quickly satisfied, for Esther simply invited the king and Haman to a banquet she'd arranged for them later that day. The king readily agreed. Esther had done admirably.

Whatever our need, we have a right to approach God with our request. Clothed in the righteousness of Christ, we can stand in His presence, assured because of Jesus' blood that we are accepted.[8] Esther touched the tip of the king's extended scepter, as if to say, "I recognize that you alone have power to execute justice in the realm." A scepter of justice is the scepter of God's kingdom.[9] We have authority as we pray to touch that scepter, to claim the overthrow of wickedness and the triumph of God's kingdom.

It had been thirty days since Esther had seen the king. She took this opportunity to prepare what would please him so he would appreciate her company. She didn't bombard him with her troubles as soon as he arrived. He had been busy with affairs of state, so she gave him time to unwind. She felt God leading her to wait yet another day.

As King Xerxes relaxed over dinner, he again assured Esther that whatever she wanted would be granted. Esther replied that if the king and Haman would come to another sumptuous banquet the next day, she would make her request then. Buoyed by King Xerxes' assurances, Esther was confident her prayers would be answered.

Esther must have longed to put this difficult situation behind her. But God enabled her to exercise patience and self-control, and to carefully choose her words. That wasn't easy when she sat near Haman and had to be a gracious hostess.

The two men departed after an uneventful but enjoyable evening. Haman was proud that he alone had been singled out to join the king and queen on this intimate occasion. The king was satisfied things were going well in the empire, and he was proud of the queen he had chosen. Little did either man realize what an eventful night would follow. It would be a night of divine intervention in state affairs.

Esther herself didn't know why she had to wait another day before disclosing her request. But one impatient word or over-anxious reaction could have spoiled God's plan. Esther would soon see the reward of her obedience. Just one more puzzle piece was necessary to complete the picture.

STUDY QUESTIONS
BE PREPARED

No one likes to be caught unprepared. Many women like to keep a meal in the freezer and extra groceries in the cupboard for unexpected guests. But do we have any spiritual reserves with which to deal with a sudden crisis?

1. List the ways in which Esther was prepared to meet her crisis.
2. Read Psalm 62:1. What aspect of prayer did Esther demonstrate that is easily neglected in our busy lifestyles? (The Living Bible translation reads: "I stand silently before the Lord, waiting for him to rescue me.")
3. Waiting on God doesn't mean inactivity. What should our attitude be, and what can we expect to receive? See Psalm 33:20; Psalm 130:5-6; and Micah 7:7.

4. What else happens when, like Esther, we take time to tune in to God and listen? See Isaiah 64:4 and Isaiah 40:31. The New King James Version translates the latter verse: "but those who *wait* on the Lord . . . ."

5. Luke 10:38-42 describes two sisters. One chose to be a listener. What hindered her sister and often hinders us from making the same choice?

6. Esther not only prayed but fasted as well. What instructions did Jesus give His disciples on fasting? See Matthew 6:16-18. Why should we fast? How does it prepare us?

13

DIVINE DELIVERANCE

Do not be afraid or discouraged because of this vast army. For the battle is not yours, but God's . . . . You will not have to fight this battle. Take up your positions; stand firm and see the deliverance the Lord will give you.

2 Chronicles 20:15-17

A prophet of God spoke these words to King Jehoshaphat as a huge force was poised to attack Judah. The king sought the Lord and proclaimed a fast for the nation, and God delivered His people.

Now, in Esther's day, God was about to do it again. Esther didn't need to fight but simply to act like the queen she was and obey her instructions. Her enemy Haman wasn't even aware a battle was raging. After all, an invitation to a banquet was hardly a challenge to fight.

How would God intervene to save His people? By mustering a great army? No. He chose to use a godly woman. In her weakness, she would shame an evil man in his strength. God didn't turn Esther into a female Samson, but He anointed her with His power. Thus equipped, what mighty task did Esther perform? She prepared a banquet.

Then what? God led her to prepare another splendid banquet. Then, as Esther was waiting patiently, the king had a sleepless night. Perhaps he'd overindulged at the dinner. Nothing seemed to help his insomnia as much as reading a book about the events of his reign. He picked up the book. By divine coincidence, his eyes lighted on the account of the foiled assassination plot.

It was another reminder of how well he'd done by choosing Esther. It was she who had brought him news of the scheme. But what about the man who first discovered it, Mordecai? There was no mention of him getting any reward. The king's attendants confirmed that nothing had been done for him, so the king decided to rectify this at once.

Meanwhile, Haman had gathered his wife and friends to gloat. He boasted that he was rich, famous, and powerful, and that he had dined alone with the king and queen. But one dark cloud remained on his horizon. All his successes gave him no satisfaction as long as a Jew named Mordecai refused to bow to him. "Why wait?" his friends asked. "Have a gallows built, seventy-five feet high, and ask the king in the morning to have Mordecai hanged on it. Then go with the king to the dinner and be happy."[1] He thought it a fine idea.

After the gallows was erected, Haman walked into the outer court just at the perfect moment. He encountered Xerxes, who asked, "What should be done for a man the king delights to honor?"

Haman thought the king had him in mind. He suggested the king clothe the man in royal garments and put him on the king's horse. Then, Haman advised that a noble prince lead the honored man through the city streets while the prince shouted: "This is what is done for the man the king delights to honor."

"Go at once," the king commanded Haman. "Get the robe and the horse and do just as you have suggested for Mordecai the Jew."[2]

Haman's face must have been quite a picture. He had been trapped by his own pride, caught up in divinely controlled circumstances. There was no escape. He was forced to carry out the king's orders and publicly honor the man he loathed. The tide had turned. Thoroughly humiliated, Haman rushed home to pour out his tale of woe.

Human reasoning could not have planned this amazing sequence of events. God's ways are far beyond ours.[3] If Esther had lain awake that night, she couldn't have imagined how God was already at work. Behind the scenes God was doing marvelous things for Esther and her people. Nothing is too difficult for Him. Mordecai's uncompromising stand wasn't an unfortunate predicament, but was God's way of forcing the enemy into the open.

It was a very subdued Haman who hurried to the second banquet. Esther arranged another delicious feast, and the king was in a generous mood. He urged her to state her request because he was ready to grant it. Haman, completely unsuspecting, waited to hear what Esther would say.

Esther laid out the facts. First, she asked the king to save her life. She pleaded with him, if he loved her, to keep her and her people from being destroyed. The king didn't question her statements. He had never had cause to doubt her utter reliability. The thought of her life being in danger was intolerable.

"Who is he?" the king demanded. "Where is the man who has dared to do such a thing?"

He was angry.

Esther didn't mince words.   "The adversary and enemy is this vile Haman," she said. Terrified, Haman pleaded desperately with her to save his life. This only infuriated the king all the more. His servants suggested punishing him on the same gallows Haman had built for Mordecai.

"Hang him on it," the king ordered. Thus, with this twist of irony, the mighty enemy was defeated.

That same day, King Xerxes gave Esther authority to do whatever she wished with Haman's estate. She didn't grab it greedily for herself. Instead, she introduced Mordecai to her husband and explained who he was. Then she set Mordecai over Haman's estate. What better man could the king find to fill the new vacancy than the one who had saved his life? The king gave Mordecai his signet ring, placed a large gold crown on his head, robed him in fine purple linen, and appointed him to a high position.

This was a day of heady triumph for Esther. But she didn't give way to pride; she recognized her own limitations. God had anointed her as a powerful intercessor on behalf of her people, but that didn't mean she was qualified to manage an estate. She was content to pass the responsibility of overseeing Haman's huge estate to someone she felt was better equipped for the job.

How important it is to not go beyond the boundaries God has set for our ministry. We need to know exactly what God requires of us; then we can expect His authority and power to accomplish it. God will enlarge our borders as He sees us walking in faith and developing the gifts He has entrusted to us. Our first calling is to minister in the foundational roles of a woman: wife, mother, daughter, sister. Each role should be marked by authority, dignity, and excellence.

Esther again dared enter the king's presence, and he extended his golden scepter. Unable to restrain her tears, she pleaded with him to stop the plan to destroy her people. Confident now that she had his trust, she begged him to demonstrate his love for her by writing an order to overrule all Haman's schemes.

Tears can often be a manifestation of self-pity or a dramatic attempt to twist a loved one's arm. But there was no ulterior motive in Esther's emotional plea. She had petitioned the king the first time without any tears or drama to draw attention to herself. Now her heart was full of compassion for her people. She had no thought for herself.

Even though she could not restrain her tears, she still kept control of her words. She wisely didn't try to dictate what the king should do. She tactfully suggested some good ideas and urged him to do what he thought was right.

Esther was exercising her authority as an intercessor. Her loving compassion for her nation was an expression of God's heart toward them. The tender concern of a woman, used in this way, becomes a valuable tool to strengthen a man's leadership. Godly emotions are a blessing when controlled by the Holy Spirit.

Be alert to the dangers of your emotions without despising their value. Whenever I find myself indulging in a tearful "pity-party," it's a sure sign that my vision is out of focus. I've set my problem — in other words, myself — at the center of my attention. God is not in view. But the moment I focus my eyes on the Lord, I can see my problems from the right perspective.

In response to Esther's plea, the king granted permission for another edict to be sent out. This order granted the Jews in every city the right to assemble and protect themselves on the day set for their destruction. They could destroy any armed force that might attack them and plunder the property of their enemies.

Mordecai gave the orders to the royal secretaries, making sure they were written in the language of every nationality in the empire.

No one could make the excuse that they didn't understand. Then he sent the dispatches express, with couriers riding the king's fastest horses.

The news brought tremendous joy. The Jews were ecstatic as they celebrated and feasted. Many people became Jews when they saw how wondrously God had worked on their behalf. And many others thought it wise to befriend the Jews.

Life had changed for Esther. She was no longer quietly reigning in the background. Now Mordecai was in a position of authority, and she was a queen to be reckoned with, involved with the affairs of the nation. The queen was like a daughter to Mordecai; he and she would work closely together. Mordecai became increasingly powerful as his reputation spread throughout the empire.

The celebrating continued. But in the midst of it, Esther and Mordecai determined they would wipe out the wicked influence of Haman forever.

STUDY QUESTIONS
PRAYER CHANGES ALL THINGS

1. Through persistent prayer, Esther saw God bring about Haman's defeat. How are we urged to follow her example? Look up the following Scriptures, comparing different versions of the Bible: Luke 18:1; 1 Thessalonians 5:17; Colossians 1:9; and Ephesians 6:18.
2. We can pray anywhere at any time. But what did Jesus do when He prayed? See Mark 1:35. Is it important for us to do the same? Why? See Matthew 6:6.
3. How should we pray? See Hebrews 11:6 and Mark 11:22-24.
4. How can we be sure God hears us? See 1 John 3:21-22 and 1 John 5:14-15.
5. What's a major hindrance to prayer? See Mark 11:25.
6. Jesus taught His disciples much about prayer. John 15:7 and John 15:14-17 are examples. Discuss these verses and any others on prayer that you've found helpful.
7. We can be unsure of how to pray or what to pray about. How

does the Holy Spirit help us pray effectively? See Romans 8:26-27.

8. We all need encouragement to pray. How can we help one another? See Acts 4:24 and Hebrews 10:19-25.

14

CELEBRATING HIS TRIUMPH

Everywhere in Persia it was known that Haman was executed for planning the annihilation of the Jews, including Queen Esther. Mordecai, a Jew, had assumed Haman's seat of power next to the king. Then Esther persuaded the king to give the Jews every opportunity to take vengeance upon their enemies. No wonder people feared the Jews.

Everyone watched with amazement as they expressed their happiness with loud songs of triumph. Only a short while before, these same people were a pitiful sight: weeping, tearing their clothes to rags, wearing rough sackcloth. Suddenly this despised nation had become a people to be respected. Their way of life stood out in marked contrast to the wickedness around them. To everyone's astonishment, once the Jews had defeated their enemies, they simply went home. Though they had the king's permission to plunder, the Jews didn't loot everything they could lay their hands on. In fact, nothing was taken. Imagine a whole nation passing up the chance to get rich quick. Observers must have thought there was something to the Jews' religion after all.

The behavior of God's people during troubled times can make a big impact on unbelievers. What we do speaks louder than what we say. Our lives are observed far more than we realize. This is especially true when we experience sickness, grief, crisis, or emergency. That's when our faith can be seen as what brings triumph in adversity.

It wasn't just the sound of joyous praise that impressed outsiders, but the way God's people so obviously loved each other as well. All the Jewish families joined in the celebration, feasting together and exchanging gifts. And the poor Jews were not left out.

They were given gifts, and everyone made sure they had enough to eat.

Jesus said, "All men will know that you are my disciples if you love one another."[1] He knew this was the most powerful way to influence those around us.

For Esther, the experience of seeing her people liberated must have been deeply rewarding. Now she understood why God had brought her to the throne. The reality was even more wonderful than the vision.

Together with Mordecai, Esther planned to work for the welfare of the Jews. Perhaps some Jews felt apprehensive that the royal authorities might turn against them once again. Esther's task was to inspire in the people faith and confidence.

To bring this about, Mordecai sent word encouraging all the Jews in the empire to continue celebrating their deliverance every year by feasting, exchanging gifts, and providing for the poor. Esther also wrote a decree with *full authority*[2] to confirm Mordecai's instructions. The annual two-day celebration was to be called the feast of Purim. The name was taken from *pur,* or lot, because Haman had cast lots to determine when the Jews would be destroyed. The holiday was to be observed by all the generations to come. It was to be a time of great gladness, a regular reminder of when sorrow had been turned to joy, and mourning to celebration. Each generation passed to the next the story of God's wonderful deliverance. It brought hope, assurance, and fresh courage to Jewish families everywhere.

In helping establish the feast of Purim, Esther ministered faith and encouragement. Scripture advises us to encourage one another,[3] and there's no better way to encourage people than to talk about God's goodness.

It's usually the woman's role to remember birthdays and special occasions, to buy gifts and plan celebrations. Women, in general, are naturally good at remembering details. We love to recount exactly what happened at some big occasion, the joke Kate played on Uncle Bob, what little Johnny did when no one was looking. It enables us to enjoy reliving memorable events.

What better way to use this gift than to share the details of God's goodness with others? The Lord delights to overwhelm us with His love by meeting some unexpressed desire. I remember this happening when my husband and I were purchasing a house. We had casually mentioned that we wanted to have a blue carpet to go with our couch and two matching chairs. We forgot about it until we saw the right color carpet already in the house. The exact shade of blue! That might seem like a small thing, but it was a boost to our faith.

As women prepared this special banquet together each year, they were bound to talk about what God had done. There were lots of details and divine coincidences to make it a tale worth repeating. Esther knew it would be a faith-building holiday.

Every woman influences people daily by what she says. As women, we need to give our often unruly tongues afresh to God so that our natural gifts of communication might be a means of encouragement. Speak gracious words.

Do you make a habit of sharing the good things God reveals to you? Do you speak of the greatness of His love? Do you tell others about your answers to prayer? Let's talk about these things to our friends, to our children, and to those around the dinner table. This can lift the conversation and turn an uneventful hour into a time of celebration. God wants us to be a praising people; that's the best antidote for discouragement.

Once unknown and seemingly insignificant, Esther had become the most influential woman in all the empire. The result of this gentle, courageous queen exercising her authority in God can be expressed in the words of the prophet Isaiah:

> The Spirit of the Sovereign Lord is on me, because the Lord has anointed me to preach good news to the poor. He has sent me to bind up the brokenhearted, to proclaim freedom for the captives and release for the prisoners ... to bestow on them a crown of beauty ... a garment of praise instead of a spirit of despair.[4]

This is our commission as women. Few of us will reign over a nation as Esther did. But we are all called to reign by bringing the kingdom of righteousness, peace, and joy into our homes and workplaces. Many around us are oppressed by sin and circumstance. They need to be given comfort and hope and need to be set free by the power of the gospel. There are many encouraging signs today that the

Holy Spirit is at work. Lives are being transformed by the power of Christ. Miracles are being seen in some parts of the world, and some nations are experiencing a mighty harvest of souls. In the People's Republic of China, for example, millions of people have entered the kingdom in recent decades.

Queen Esther's story isn't some romantic tale out of the Arabian Nights. It's from the Word of God. The Bible says of itself that all Scripture is God-breathed — divinely inspired — and useful for teaching, so that the men and women of God may be thoroughly equipped for every good work.[5] Esther's story is thrilling. But we must not allow ourselves to enjoy the plot, praise God for its joyous ending, then push it to the dusty closets of our minds. It's not to be disregarded as ancient history. It's a message for today.

God is building a triumphant church across the globe, and nothing will prevail against it. He wants to raise up a generation of men and women with a vision to accomplish all that He has for them. The kingdom of this world shall become the kingdom of our God.[6] Just as Esther fulfilled God's purpose in her generation, you, too, have been called to be a woman of authority and to fulfill your kingdom destiny.

Perhaps you don't understand what that means for you. Esther didn't fully understand either as she took that first trusting step and obeyed God's call. But her mission unfolded as she walked in submission to God, and she discovered that the beauty of her willing spirit became her greatest asset. The vision of one day being queen enabled her to set her heart on fulfilling God's purpose for her life.

Totally committing yourself to God's will and ways is the pathway to glorious freedom and fulfillment. Once you step out in faith and obedience, the beauty of Christ will be yours.

Queen, take your throne!

STUDY QUESTIONS
LOVE ONE ANOTHER

Esther demonstrated her love for her people in a practical way. All Christians are called to show their love for each other by deeds as well as by words. Read 1 John 3:16-18 and 1 John 4:7-12,16,19, 20.

1. What practical examples are given of what it means to show love to one another? How did God show His love for us? How are we able to love as God does?
2. How did the people in the early church express their love? See Acts 4:32-35.
3. Find other examples to follow in Romans 12:13; Philemon 22; and 1 Timothy 5:10.
4. How should we treat our own relatives? See 1 Timothy 5:3-8.
5. How should we express our love by giving money? Read 2 Corinthians 8:1-7 and 2 Corinthians 9:7-8.
6. How did Jesus fulfill Luke 4:18?
7. Discuss practical ways in which Christian women can reach out to the poor and needy. What are women doing in your town or city? Is this everyone's calling? See Romans 12:6a. How much should you be involved? Perhaps you can do this one thing: Pray for the needy people where you live and for those who minister to them.

15

THE KING'S HANDIWORK

So you've come this far. You've read about becoming a woman of authority, a queen in God's kingdom. What's your response? Perhaps you can identify with some of these women.

Janet: "Of course I want to be a beautiful woman, someone worthy of being a queen. But I know I haven't made it. I guess there's a lot of purifying still to be done. I need to speed up the beauty process by exercising some self-discipline and humility. I'll take a long look into my heart and ferret out all my unconfessed sins. I hope I can remember everything. Then I'll vow never to repeat the same mistakes."

Jeanne: "I'm determined to behave like a woman of authority in this crisis that's hit my family. Esther fasted for three days. I've never missed more than one meal, but here goes. No food for three days. Why do I keep thinking about luscious meals? You'd think I was planning a feast rather than trying to hear God speak to me. It's tough to pray when your tummy keeps rumbling and the children come home as ravenous as ever. I'll never make an intercessor. Someone else must have been chosen for a time such as this."

Betty: "Never again will I see womanhood as a limitation. The things women do are just as valuable as what men do. From now on, I'm going to cut out everything I like that's a man's job and concentrate on women's projects. I'm good at arranging flowers. What? Pete is a florist? Then I'll join the catering team. Jeff leads the catering team? Help! What is there for a woman to do?"

Susan: "I want everyone to know I have a meek and quiet spirit without having to tell them. Help me to show it on the outside, Lord! Just to prove I genuinely want to change, I'll start by changing my wardrobe. That's something I know I can do. Those brilliantly colored pants of mine have got to go. Esther wouldn't have looked right in them. Too bad. They were such a bargain. Most of my clothes are bold colors. Shouldn't I switch to more subdued shades? Perhaps I could occasionally indulge in a striking accessory . . . ."

Sherry: "I wish I could believe it. But how can there be a throne for me? Time and time again I let the Lord down and give way to temptation. At times I feel totally ashamed of myself. But it's no good pretending to be what I'm not. If I'd been living in Esther's situation, I know I would have been unable to stop myself from over-eating at banquets and otherwise indulging myself. I can even see myself joining heathens in their sin just to be accepted and popular. That's what I was like before I was saved, and sometimes I think I'll never change."

All these imaginary women have been looking in the wrong place for their thrones. We need to continually remind ourselves that the throne we're to occupy is in God's kingdom of grace. Our attention needs to focus on God's work in us, not on our own efforts to change. Our success will be found not by striving but by God's grace. Grace is an undeserved gift. It's the unmerited favor, power, and excellence freely bestowed on us by God. Esther lived in a kingdom where the rule of law prevailed, yet she obtained favor by the grace of God that was upon her. That's how she came to the throne.

As you look at Esther and learn the lessons on how to be a queen, don't make the mistake of trying to work it all out by establishing your own "I should" list. Beware of the trap of creating a new set of rules to keep in order to become women of authority. God doesn't want us to afflict ourselves with lists, dress codes, rigorous bouts of fasting, or with becoming extremely introspective. Setting up a self-imposed discipline program is a good way to lock yourself up in Condemnation Castle.

Neither will you find freedom if, like Betty, you carefully stick to tasks you think are exclusively a woman's domain. Other women pride themselves in being able to do what was once considered a man's job. These things are not the issue. Our identity as women will be found in Christ, not in the tasks we do.

Like Sherry above, so many women write themselves off,

certain they will never make the throne. You might feel disappointed at your failures, but God will never give up on you. He will keep working in your heart.

To apply the lessons of this Old Testament story, we must look for the revelation God has given us in the New. There we find that we were saved by grace through faith.[1] We can continue to live in Christ in the same way.

The moment we were saved we came under a new master. Sin shall not be your master, Scripture says, because you are not under law, but under grace.[2] Every time you feel disappointed at your failures, it's proof that the grace of God is at work. If sin were really still our master, we would never feel bad about sinning. But because grace is our master, we feel shame. We have been set free from sin and have become slaves to righteousness.[3] To become queens, we must take our place in this righteous kingdom where grace reigns. "For if," Paul says, "by the trespass of the one man [Adam], death reigned through that one man, how much more will those who receive God's abundant provision of grace and of the gift of righteousness reign in life through the one man, Jesus Christ."[4] When you totally submit your life to the lordship of Christ, you take your place with Him, reigning in every situation.

It's the grace of God that teaches you to say no to temptation.[5] It's the grace of God that produces a meek and quiet spirit. It's the grace of God that enables you to enjoy being the woman God intended you to be. Grace is available to you in every crisis, and it will abound in you so you can be a blessing to others.

That's the way you will find your throne. When we look at what the New Testament teaches about what it means to reign, we see that the message of Esther is an attainable reality, not just a tantalizing dream.

STUDY QUESTIONS
GRACE: ALL WE NEED

We've no reason to boast. We were saved by grace through faith. Now we live and reign in the same way. It's good to remind ourselves of the abundant supply of grace that is ours in Christ.

1. How and when do we receive it? See Hebrews 4:16.
2. We are not saved by works, but once saved, we have a job to do. Paul explains in 1 Corinthians 15:10 how he succeeded. This will also be the secret of our success.
3. Look at how Paul mentioned grace at the beginning and end of each of his epistles: Romans, 1 and 2 Corinthians, Galatians, Ephesians, Philippians, Colossians, 1 and 2 Thessalonians, 1 and 2 Timothy, Titus, and Philemon. Did he expect this would make a difference in the way people lived? How?
4. Read Titus 2:11-14. What kind of people will be ready to meet Jesus when He comes again? What part does grace play in our preparation?
5. How does God's Word describe our supply of grace? See John 1:16; Acts 4:33; Romans 5:17; Ephesians 2:7; and 1 Timothy 1:14.
6. What will dry up the supply of God's grace? What will cause it to flow? See James 4:6-7a.
7. Read 2 Peter 3:18. How will grace enable you to make spiritual progress.

16

THE WOMAN OF AUTHORITY

So, then, who is a queen? Who is this woman of authority that God calls us to become?

In sum, she is a woman who has a relationship with the Father. Through that relationship she recognizes she is valued. She lives with the confidence that she is a chosen woman. No matter what circumstances she encounters, she knows God has a plan for her life, and that it's good. She pursues her call to authority under the direction of a local church, where she can be accountable and effective in ministry, and can display God's majesty through her relationships in a loving community. She believes that God is going to give her all the spiritual equipment — authority — she'll need to fulfill her destiny.

She doesn't have to be married to a pastor, have a high-powered job, or lead a dynamic ministry. A woman whose life consists mainly of doing ordinary tasks around the home is equally valuable in God's kingdom. Her worth comes from who she is, not from what she does. She knows as a woman of God that she is of incalculable worth even as she serves Him in the most mundane chores.

Someone who is really moving in authority is reigning in her ordinary circumstances. She's coping. She's improving. She's not overwhelmed by circumstances. She exhibits the glory of belonging to God's kingdom by the way in which she lives. A woman of authority makes God's teaching attractive. Everything she does demonstrates something: who she is, who she serves, that she's part of something worthwhile.

A woman's authority isn't rulership. It's functioning in her God-given abilities in a way that demonstrates God's authority. The authority given to the women of God will not threaten men. It will enhance and strengthen them. When women take their rightful place, men will be released and inspired to take their proper role. Esther was an asset to the king, not a threat.

A woman of authority has a heart that embraces humility and obedience. She doesn't see submission as an inhibiting straitjacket. Rather, it's by carrying out the King's commands that she exercises her authority. Through this, she can function at her best and fulfill her highest potential. Christ, who submitted to His Father in everything, manifested all the greatness of the Godhead.

Submission in no way suggests that women have an inferior status. No one — man or woman — has any authority in the kingdom except the authority Christ has delegated. Men and women alike are called to follow His supreme example of submission.

Esther received authority the moment the king placed a crown on her head. From then on, she exercised authority in everything she did. Whether she was doing routine tasks or making momentous decisions, being a woman of authority became a way of life. She exercised the same authority on an uneventful day as during a major crisis. The only difference was that greater challenges required greater faith.

Esther's crown and clothing symbolized the authority that came from her relationship to the king. But on informal occasions when she wasn't wearing her royal garb, no one would refuse to carry out her wishes. The inner beauty that had won her the king's favor still shone from within her. It was undeniable evidence that this was the woman entrusted with the crown.

Whenever you act in a way that demonstrates who your King really is, you put on your uniform of authority. You need no badge saying, "Woman of Authority at Work." People will realize that the source of your authority is not you, but Christ and His grace working in you.

WORDS OF AUTHORITY

Peter tells wives that they can win their unbelieving husbands to Christ by exercising authority. How? By using powerful words designed to dispel doubts, convict him of sin, and prove that the wife is right? No. By showing their husbands the beauty of a woman clothed with a meek and quiet spirit. That's the way to bring God's authority into a situation and see prayers answered. It requires faith, patience, and an abundance of God's grace. But it never fails to get results.

Our behavior can speak louder than words. But the Bible doesn't say women should never open their mouths. Communication is necessary to advance the kingdom. Paul's exhortation to Timothy is also applicable to women: "Preach the Word; be prepared in season and out of season; correct, rebuke and encourage."[1] And Peter tells us:

> But in your hearts set apart Christ as Lord. Always be prepared to give an answer to everyone who asks you to give the reason for the hope that you have. But do this with gentleness and respect.[2]

Our words will have authority if we have a gentle spirit, not if we win our arguments.

AUTHORITY IN MINISTRY

Taking your place on the throne allows you to function in the local church in a new dimension. We have authority in Christ to preach the good news and to make disciples of all nations. Women can step out in ministry, confident that Jesus will use them to build His church. This is the New Testament pattern. In his letter to the Romans, Paul expressed his appreciation for the women who labored with him. He commended Phoebe, Priscilla, Mary, Tryphena, Tryphosa, and Persis as those who worked hard for the Lord.[3]

We have different gifts, according to the grace given us.[4] Just as each part of your body has a function, so every woman has a gift, or function, as a member of the body of Christ. The whole body can work more effectively when you do your assignments as a queen, taking your rightful place in God's house. The list of opportunities is endless: hospitality, helping, encouraging, giving, showing mercy, mothering, counseling, discipling, teaching other women, evangelizing, exercising spiritual gifts.

AUTHORITY IN PRAYER

Queen Esther's key role was intercession. Praying was her most critical task in her hour of destiny. She entered the presence of the great King to seek His intervention on behalf of her people.

Is your prayer life just a shopping list of requests? Or do you approach the throne of God expecting to release His power and authority in the lives of those for whom you pray? Scripture says that Jesus ever lives to intercede[5] and that He is our great High Priest.[6] We have been chosen as royal priests[7] and can exercise that authority in prayer. We all know of situations that require God's intervention. We can learn from Esther, who gathered her servants around her to pray and fast. It's much more encouraging to pray with a group that shares your burden.

When you take your place on the throne, you begin a process of learning to reign. As Esther clearly demonstrated, this involves learning to exert authority as well as developing a meek and quiet spirit. The two go hand-in-hand. The encouraging message of the New Testament is that the grace of God has already begun this process within us. You can be a queen and yet continue learning more about this inner beauty every day.

Esther had no regrets about becoming queen. Neither will you. As you begin walking in the reality of who you are as God's chosen woman, you will demonstrate that Christ is truly reigning. Esther experienced the thrill of seeing her enemy Haman defeated. You will experience the thrill of seeing Satan defeated and the joy of playing your vital part in the triumph of God's kingdom.

STUDY QUESTIONS
CLOTHING FIT FOR A QUEEN

A woman's clothing often gives away her nationality; a Christian woman's clothing should be an indication of the kingdom to which she belongs. Let's look for scriptural guidelines that can help us make choices on proper attire.

1. How do the characteristics of the kingdom of God found in

Romans 14:17 relate to our inner and outer appearance?

2. Discuss the spiritual garments described in Isaiah 61:3,10.

3. What spiritual clothing demonstrates peace and harmony? See 1 Peter 3:4 and 1 Peter 5:5.

4. What other clothing is essential for a Christian? See Luke 24:49.

5. Read Proverbs 31:25; Matthew 6:28-33; and 1 Timothy 2:9-10. How can these verses be applied practically? How should they affect our attitude in deciding what to wear?

6. Scripture speaks of our future wedding day. What garments do we need? See Revelation 19:7-8. What will it be like when the daughters of the King of Kings enter His palace? See Psalm 45:7-15.

NOTES

Chapter 2. REVOLT REVEALED

1. Exod. 17:4
2. 1 Sam. 15:23, NKJ

Chapter 3. THE LIBERATED WOMAN

1. Gen 3:6
2. 1 Kings 11:4
3. Judg. 4:14
4. 2 Tim 1:5
5. 1 Peter 3:1-2
6. Heb. 5:7
7. John 5:19

Chapter 4. MADE MAJESTIC TOGETHER

1. Eph. 2:7
2. 1 Peter 2:9 (italics added)
3. Heb. 10:25
4. 1 Cor. 12:27
5. John 3:18
6. John 17:20-21
7. John 17:21
8. Gen. 2:18, 20-24
9. Prov. 18:22
10. Prov. 31:12

Chapter 5. FINDING YOUR PLACE

1. Judg. 4:4-9
2. Col. 3:23-24

Chapter 6. ADVERSITY NO OBSTACLE

1. Rom. 8:28
2. Psalm 139:16
3. Eph. 1:11 and Rom. 12:2

Chapter 7. FROM PRISON TO PRIVILEGE

1. Gal. 3:26-28
2. Matt. 25:23
3. Col. 3:23-24

Chapter 8. BORN-AGAIN BEAUTY

1. 2 Cor. 5:17
2. Gal 2:20
3. Luke 24:49
4. Josh. 1:8
5. Eph. 1:4
6. 1 Thess. 5:23-24
7. Titus 2:14
8. Heb. 12:11

Chapter 9. A NEW LOOK

1. 1 Peter 3:3-4
2. 2 Cor. 5:17
3. Gal. 3:27
4. Matt. 11:29, NKJ
5. 2 Peter 1:3-4
6. Rom. 13:14
7. 2 Cor. 2:15
8. Matt. 11:29
9. Phil. 2:13
   (italics added)
10. Titus 2:10

Chapter 10. TAKING THE THRONE

1. 2 Cor. 4:7
2. 1 Tim. 3:11
3. Prov. 31:30
4. Prov. 31:15-20
5. Prov. 8:13
6. Psalm 16:8
7. Prov. 31:11-12
8. Prov. 31:25
9. Matt. 28:18
10. Luke 24:49
11. Acts 2:38-39
12. Eph. 1:13-14
13. John 16:7
14. John 16:13-14
15. Rom. 8:26
16. Luke 11:13

Chapter 11. PUT TO THE TEST

1. Exod. 17:14
2. Esther 4:14

Chapter 12. THE QUEEN IN CRISIS

1. Luke 9:23-24
2. Rom. 13:1
3. Acts 5:29
4. Esther 4:16
5. Matt. 6:16
6. Arthur Wallis, God's Chosen Fast (Fort Washington: Christian Literature Crusade, 1968), p. 105.
7. Esther 5:3
8. Heb. 10:19
9. Psalm 45:6

Chapter 13. DIVINE DELIVERANCE

1. Esther 5:14
2. Esther 6:10
3. Isa. 55:9

Chapter 14. CELEBRATING HIS TRIUMPH

1. John 13:35
2. Esther 9:29
3. Heb. 10:25
4. Isa. 61:1-3
5. 2 Tim. 3:16
6. Rev. 11:15

Chapter 15. THE KING'S HANDIWORK

1. Eph. 2:8-9
2. Rom. 6:14
3. Rom. 6:18
4. Rom. 5:17
5. Titus 2:11-12

Chapter 16. THE WOMAN OF AUTHORITY

1. 2 Tim. 4:2
2. 1 Peter 3:15-16
3. Rom.16:1,3,6,12
4. Rom. 12:6
5. Heb. 7:25
6. Heb. 7:26
7. 1 Peter 2:9